SPY BOY™

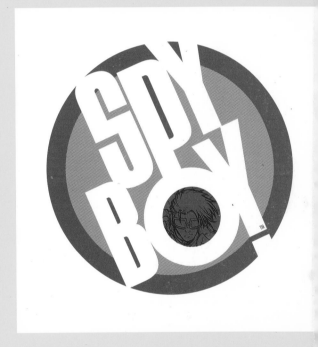

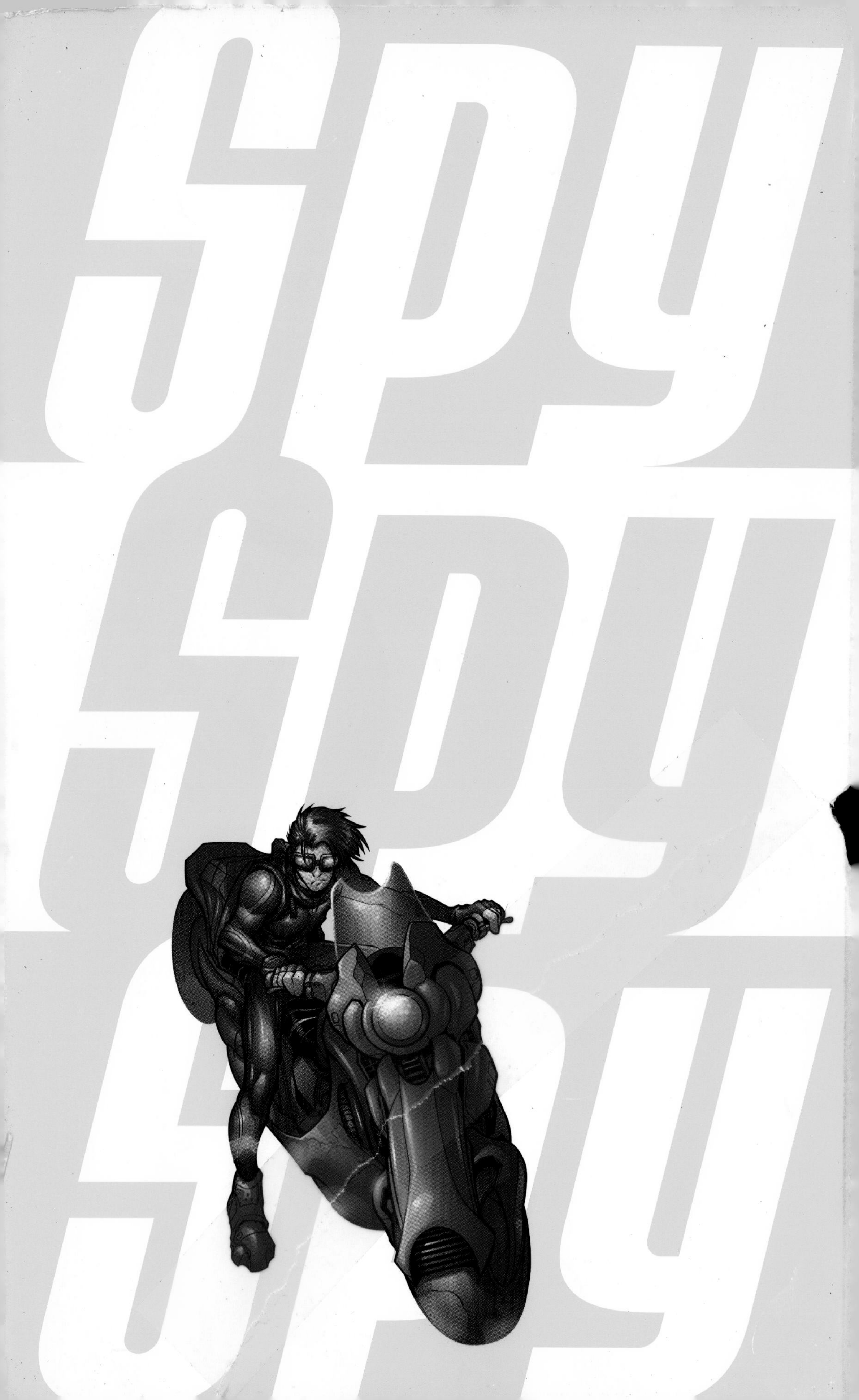
spy
spy
spy

SpyBoy

in

The Deadly Gourmet Affair

Story
Peter david

Pencils
Pop Mhan

Inks
Norman Lee

Lettering
Clem Robins

Colors
Guy Major

Dark Horse Comics

PUBLISHER
Mike Richardson

SERIES EDITOR
Phil Amara

COLLECTION EDITOR
Chris Warner

BOOK DESIGN
Mark Cox

SPYBOY™: THE DEADLY GOURMET AFFAIR

© 1999, 2001 Dark Horse Comics, Inc. Spyboy™ and all other prominent characters and their
distinctive likenesses are trademarks of Dark Horse Comics, Inc. All rights reserved. No portion of
this publication may be reproduced, in any form or by any means, without the express written
permission of Dark Horse Comics, Inc. Names, characters, places, and incidents featured in this
publication are either the product of the author's imagination or are used fictitiously. Any resemblance
to actual persons (living or dead), events, institutions, or locales, without satiric intent, is coincidental.
Dark Horse Comics® and the Dark Horse logo are trademarks of Dark Horse Comics, Inc., registered
in various categories and countries. All rights reserved.

This volume collects issues one through three of the Dark Horse comic-book series *SpyBoy.*

Published by
Dark Horse Comics, Inc.
10956 S.E. main Street
Milwaukie, OR 97222

www.darkhorse.com

To find a comics shop in your area, call the Comic Shop Locator Service toll-free at 1-888-266-4226

First edition: January 2001
ISBN: 1-56971-463-0

10 9 8 7 6 5 4 3 2
Printed in China

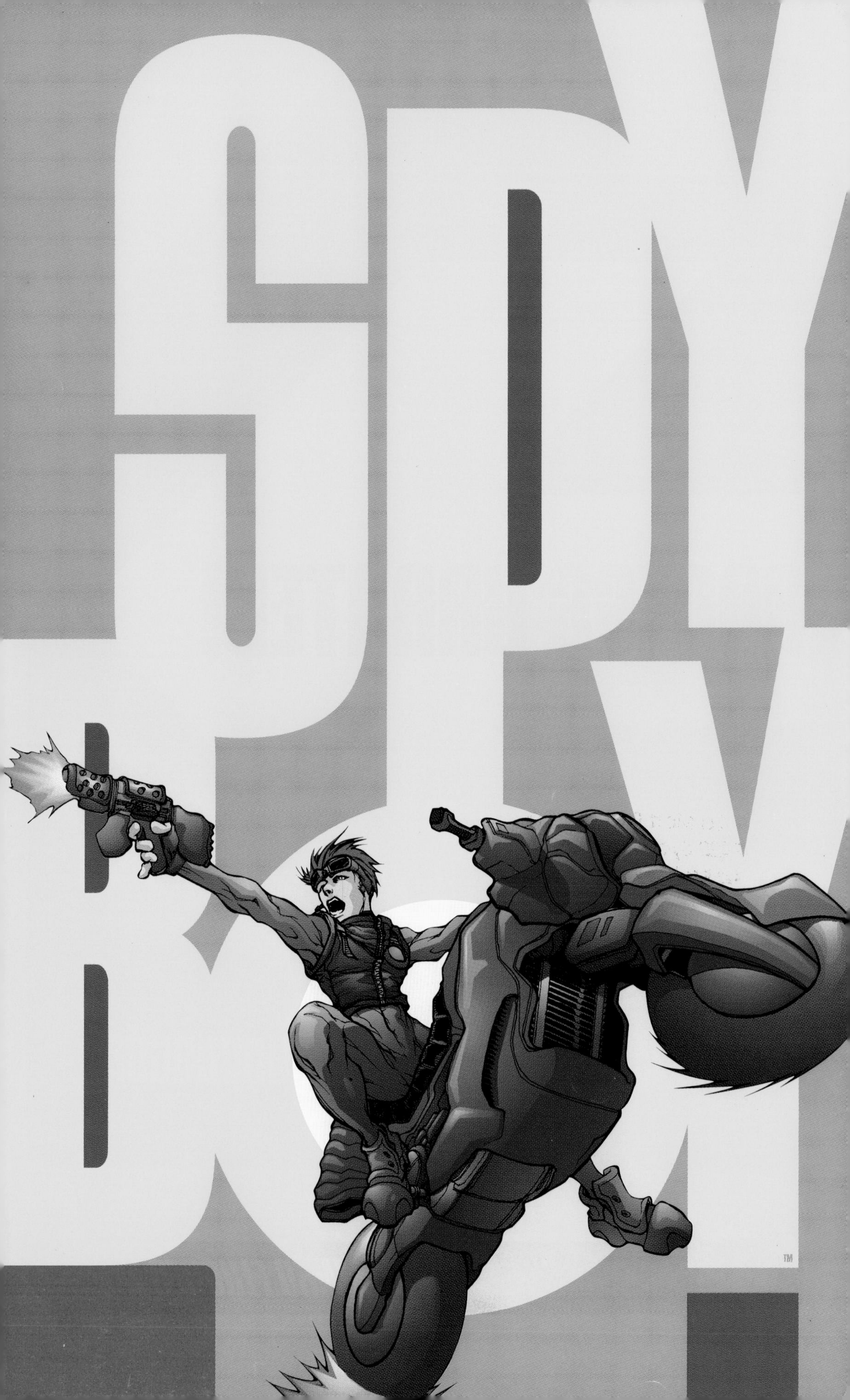
SPY BOY™

ACCESS GRANTED!

THIS WAY FOR MAXIMUM ADVENTURE

1

"THE SPY WHO FLUSHED ME"

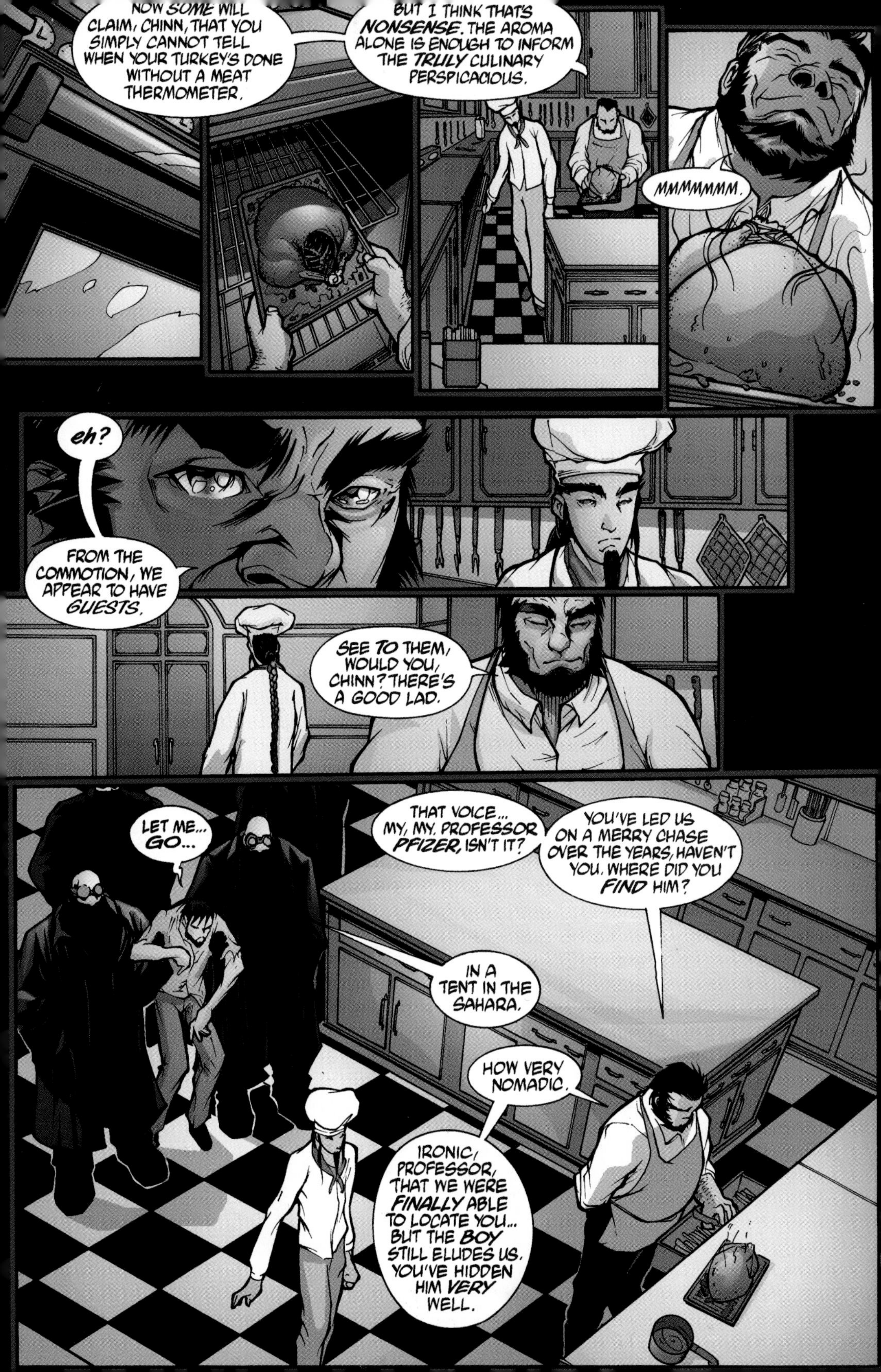
NOW SOME WILL CLAIM, CHINN, THAT YOU SIMPLY CANNOT TELL WHEN YOUR TURKEY'S DONE WITHOUT A MEAT THERMOMETER.
BUT I THINK THAT'S NONSENSE. THE AROMA ALONE IS ENOUGH TO INFORM THE TRULY CULINARY PERSPICACIOUS.
MMMMMMM.
eh?
FROM THE COMMOTION, WE APPEAR TO HAVE GUESTS.
SEE TO THEM, WOULD YOU, CHINN? THERE'S A GOOD LAD.
LET ME... GO...
THAT VOICE... MY, MY, PROFESSOR PFIZER, ISN'T IT?
YOU'VE LED US ON A MERRY CHASE OVER THE YEARS, HAVEN'T YOU. WHERE DID YOU FIND HIM?
IN A TENT IN THE SAHARA.
HOW VERY NOMADIC.
IRONIC, PROFESSOR, THAT WE WERE FINALLY ABLE TO LOCATE YOU... BUT THE BOY STILL ELUDES US. YOU'VE HIDDEN HIM VERY WELL.

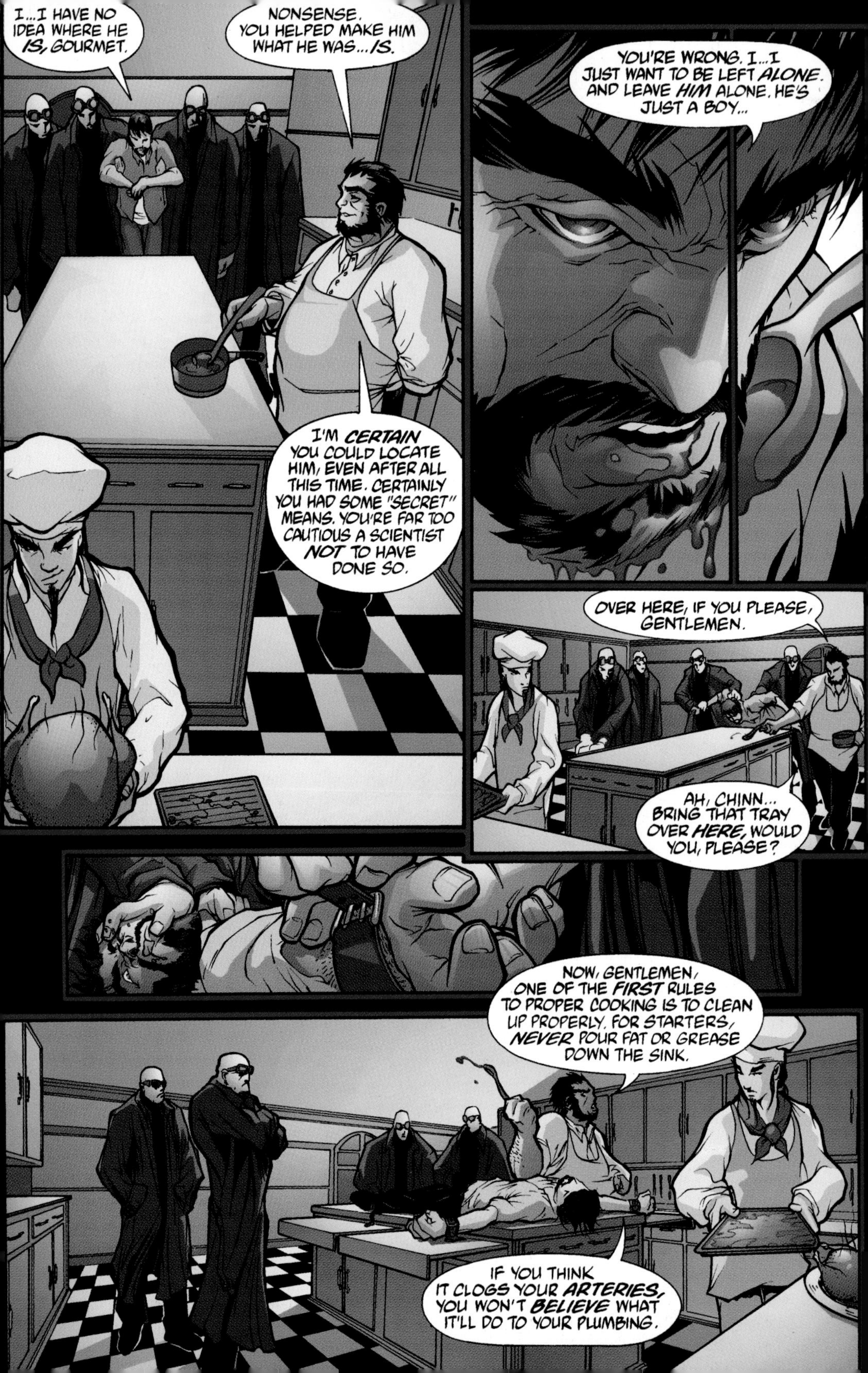
I...I HAVE NO IDEA WHERE HE IS, GOURMET.
NONSENSE. YOU HELPED MAKE HIM WHAT HE WAS... IS.
I'M CERTAIN YOU COULD LOCATE HIM, EVEN AFTER ALL THIS TIME. CERTAINLY YOU HAD SOME "SECRET" MEANS. YOU'RE FAR TOO CAUTIOUS A SCIENTIST NOT TO HAVE DONE SO.
YOU'RE WRONG. I...I JUST WANT TO BE LEFT ALONE. AND LEAVE HIM ALONE. HE'S JUST A BOY...
OVER HERE, IF YOU PLEASE, GENTLEMEN.
AH, CHINN... BRING THAT TRAY OVER HERE, WOULD YOU, PLEASE?
NOW, GENTLEMEN, ONE OF THE FIRST RULES TO PROPER COOKING IS TO CLEAN UP PROPERLY. FOR STARTERS, NEVER POUR FAT OR GREASE DOWN THE SINK.
IF YOU THINK IT CLOGS YOUR ARTERIES, YOU WON'T BELIEVE WHAT IT'LL DO TO YOUR PLUMBING.

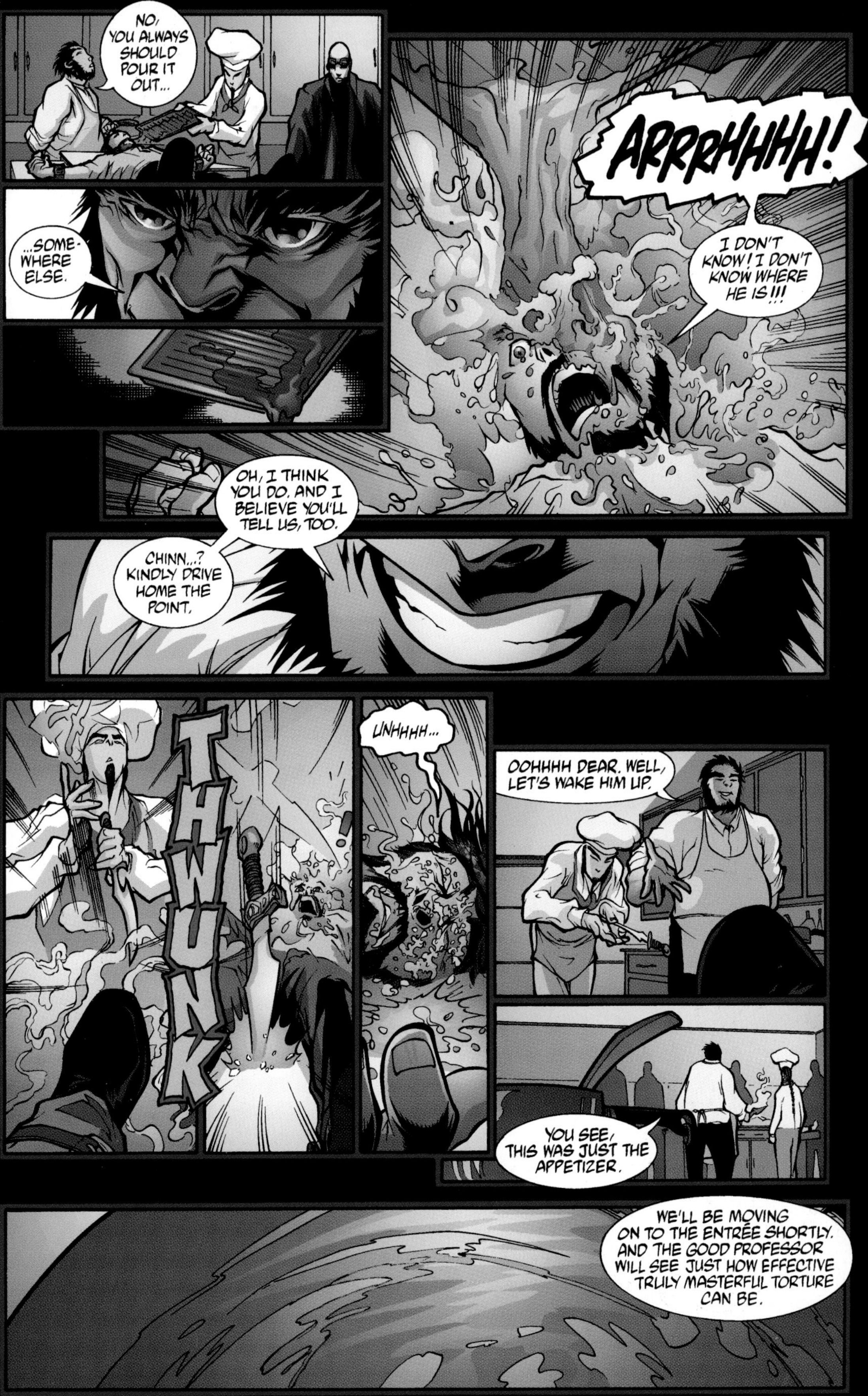
NO, YOU ALWAYS SHOULD POUR IT OUT...
...SOME-WHERE ELSE.
ARRRHHHH!
I DON'T KNOW! I DON'T KNOW WHERE HE IS!!!
OH, I THINK YOU DO, AND I BELIEVE YOU'LL TELL US, TOO.
CHINN...? KINDLY DRIVE HOME THE POINT.
THWUNK
UNHHHH...
OOHHHH DEAR. WELL, LET'S WAKE HIM UP.
YOU SEE, THIS WAS JUST THE APPETIZER.
WE'LL BE MOVING ON TO THE ENTRÉE SHORTLY. AND THE GOOD PROFESSOR WILL SEE JUST HOW EFFECTIVE TRULY MASTERFUL TORTURE CAN BE.

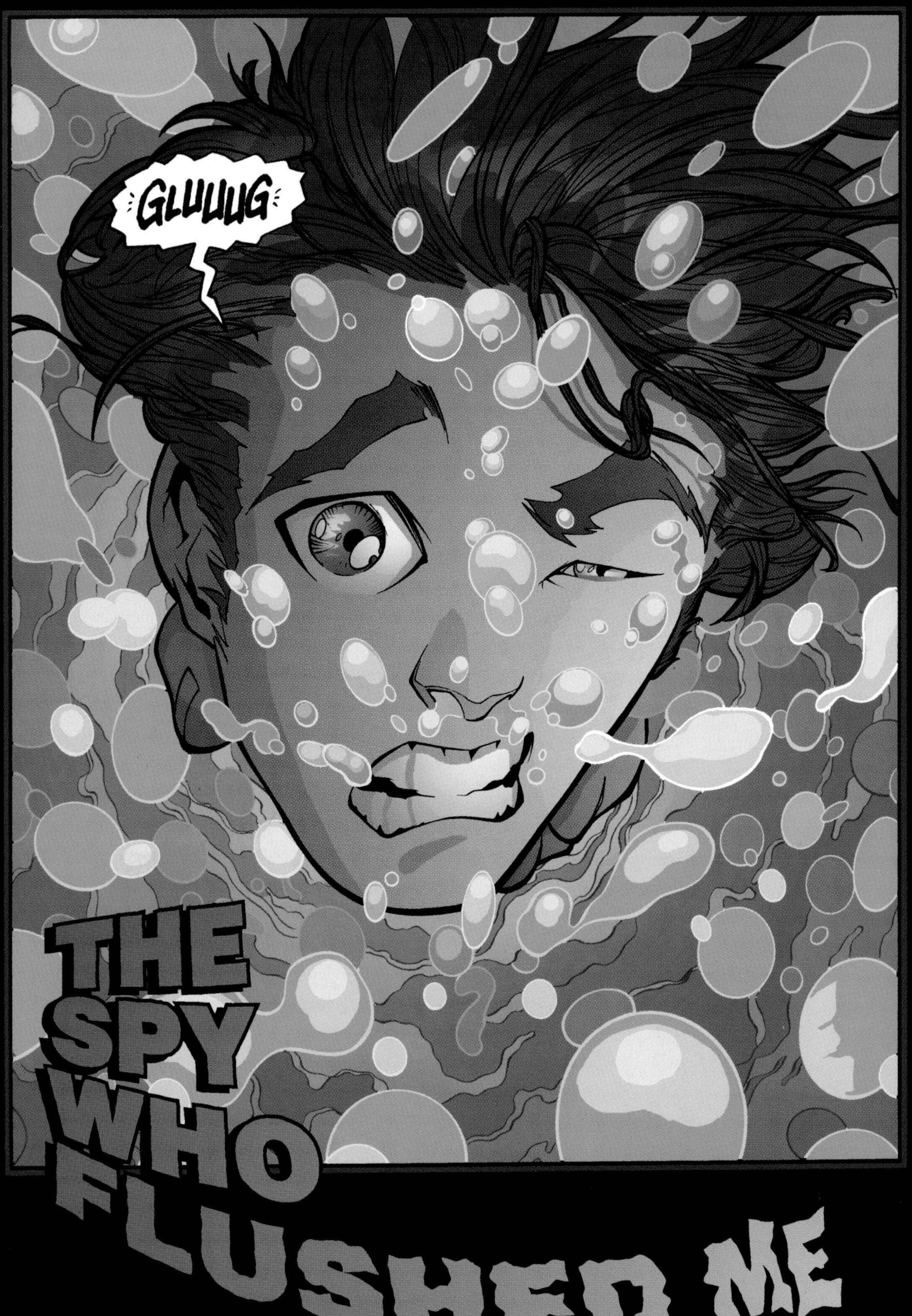
GLUUUG

THE SPY WHO FLUSHED ME

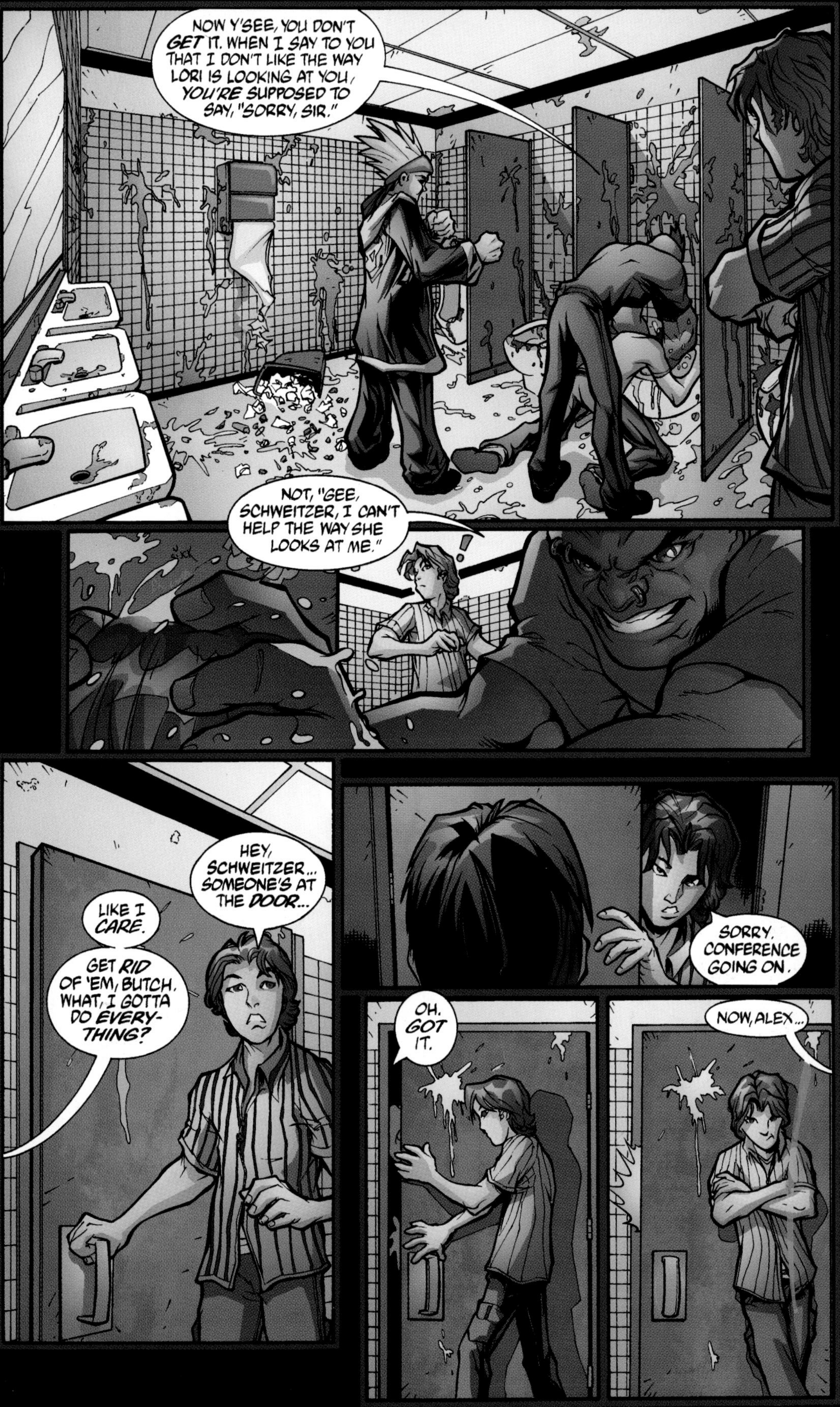
NOW Y'SEE, YOU DON'T GET IT. WHEN I SAY TO YOU THAT I DON'T LIKE THE WAY LORI IS LOOKING AT YOU, YOU'RE SUPPOSED TO SAY, "SORRY, SIR."
NOT, "GEE, SCHWEITZER, I CAN'T HELP THE WAY SHE LOOKS AT ME."
!
HEY, SCHWEITZER... SOMEONE'S AT THE DOOR...
LIKE I CARE.
GET RID OF 'EM, BUTCH. WHAT, I GOTTA DO EVERY-THING?
SORRY. CONFERENCE GOING ON.
OH. GOT IT.
NOW, ALEX...

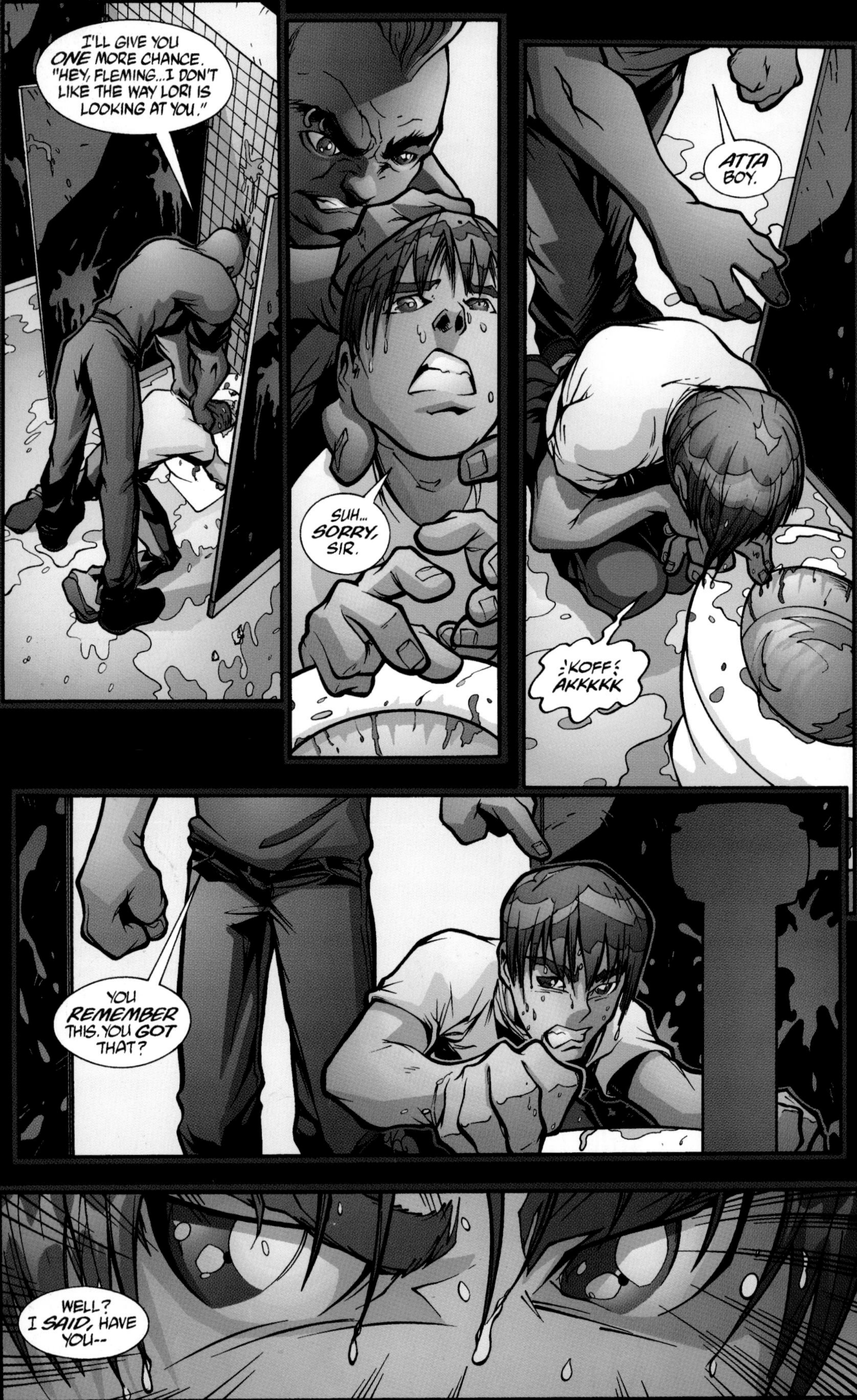
I'LL GIVE YOU ONE MORE CHANCE. "HEY, FLEMING...I DON'T LIKE THE WAY LORI IS LOOKING AT YOU."
SUH... SORRY, SIR.
ATTA BOY.
:KOFF: AKKKKK
YOU REMEMBER THIS. YOU GOT THAT?
WELL? I SAID, HAVE YOU--

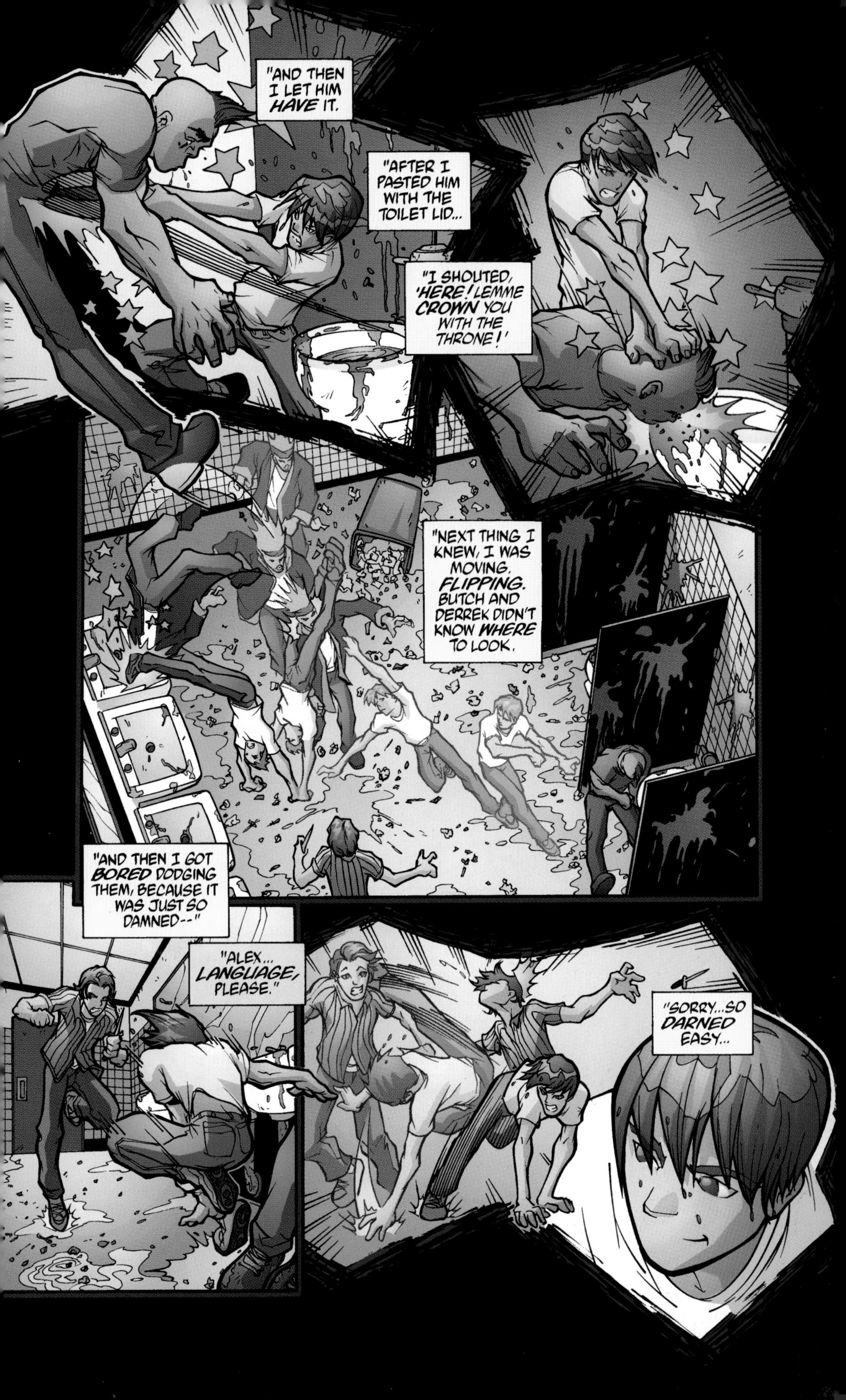
"AND THEN I LET HIM HAVE IT.
"AFTER I PASTED HIM WITH THE TOILET LID...
"I SHOUTED, 'HERE! LEMME CROWN YOU WITH THE THRONE!'
"NEXT THING I KNEW, I WAS MOVING. FLIPPING. BUTCH AND DERREK DIDN'T KNOW WHERE TO LOOK.
"AND THEN I GOT BORED DODGING THEM, BECAUSE IT WAS JUST SO DAMNED--"
"ALEX... LANGUAGE, PLEASE."
"SORRY...SO DARNED EASY...

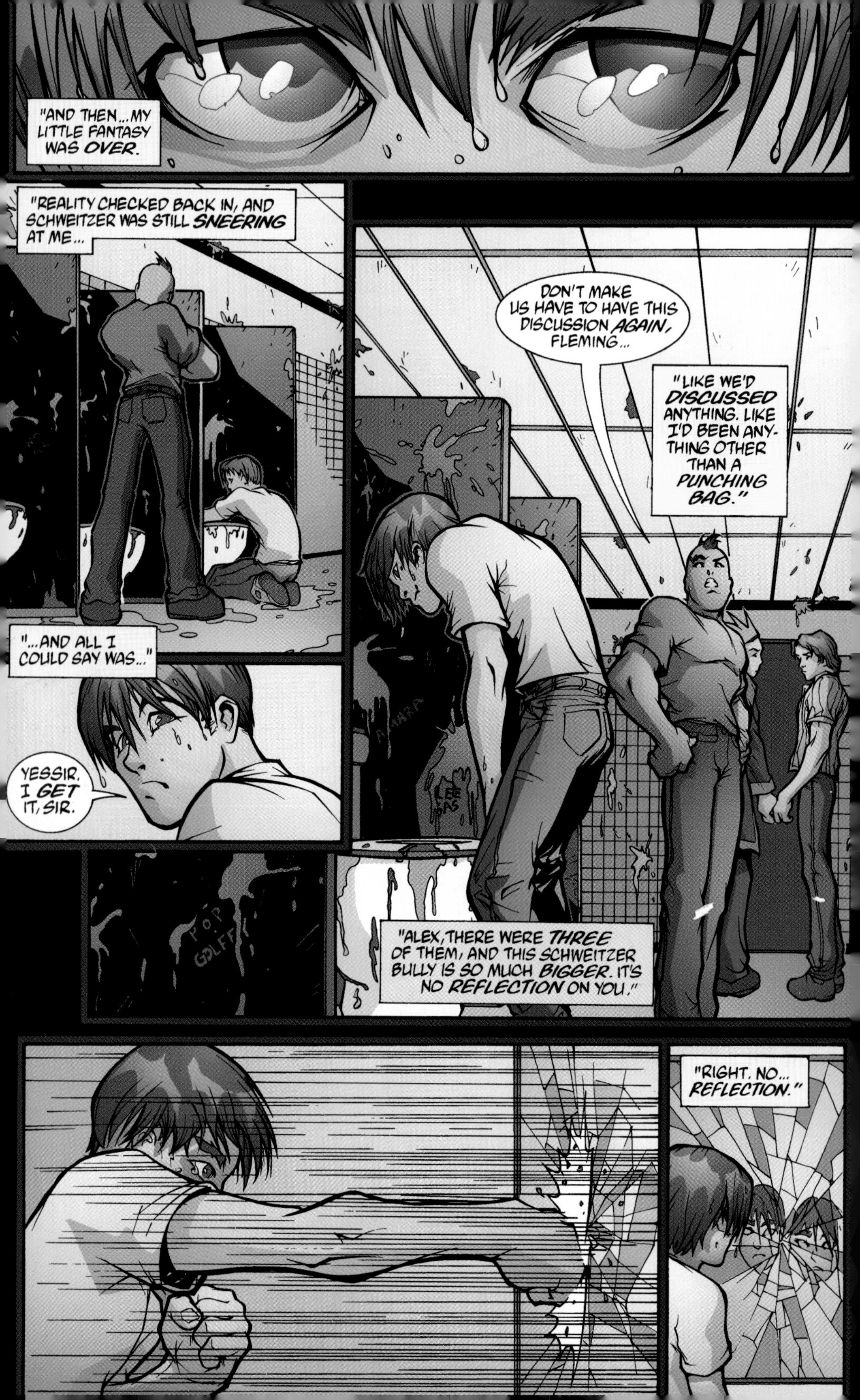
"AND THEN... MY LITTLE FANTASY WAS OVER.
"REALITY CHECKED BACK IN, AND SCHWEITZER WAS STILL SNEERING AT ME...
DON'T MAKE US HAVE TO HAVE THIS DISCUSSION AGAIN, FLEMING...
"LIKE WE'D DISCUSSED ANYTHING. LIKE I'D BEEN ANYTHING OTHER THAN A PUNCHING BAG."
"...AND ALL I COULD SAY WAS..."
YESSIR. I GET IT, SIR.
"ALEX, THERE WERE THREE OF THEM, AND THIS SCHWEITZER BULLY IS SO MUCH BIGGER. IT'S NO REFLECTION ON YOU."
"RIGHT. NO... REFLECTION."

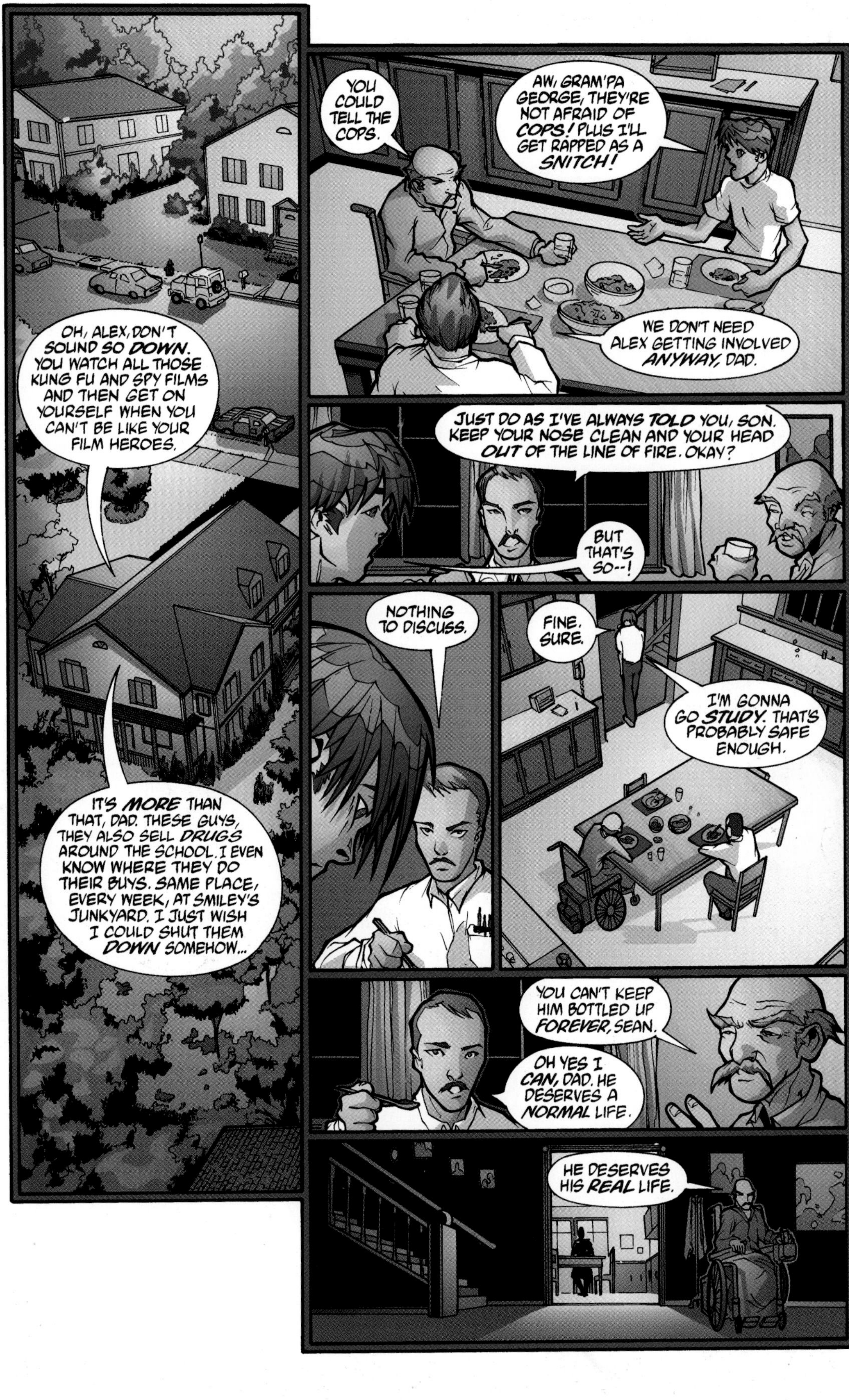
YOU COULD TELL THE COPS.
AW, GRAM'PA GEORGE, THEY'RE NOT AFRAID OF COPS! PLUS I'LL GET RAPPED AS A SNITCH!
WE DON'T NEED ALEX GETTING INVOLVED ANYWAY, DAD.
OH, ALEX, DON'T SOUND SO DOWN. YOU WATCH ALL THOSE KUNG FU AND SPY FILMS AND THEN GET ON YOURSELF WHEN YOU CAN'T BE LIKE YOUR FILM HEROES.
IT'S MORE THAN THAT, DAD. THESE GUYS, THEY ALSO SELL DRUGS AROUND THE SCHOOL. I EVEN KNOW WHERE THEY DO THEIR BUYS. SAME PLACE, EVERY WEEK, AT SMILEY'S JUNKYARD. I JUST WISH I COULD SHUT THEM DOWN SOMEHOW...
JUST DO AS I'VE ALWAYS TOLD YOU, SON. KEEP YOUR NOSE CLEAN AND YOUR HEAD OUT OF THE LINE OF FIRE. OKAY?
BUT THAT'S SO--!
NOTHING TO DISCUSS.
FINE. SURE.
I'M GONNA GO STUDY. THAT'S PROBABLY SAFE ENOUGH.
YOU CAN'T KEEP HIM BOTTLED UP FOREVER, SEAN.
OH YES I CAN, DAD. HE DESERVES A NORMAL LIFE.
HE DESERVES HIS REAL LIFE.

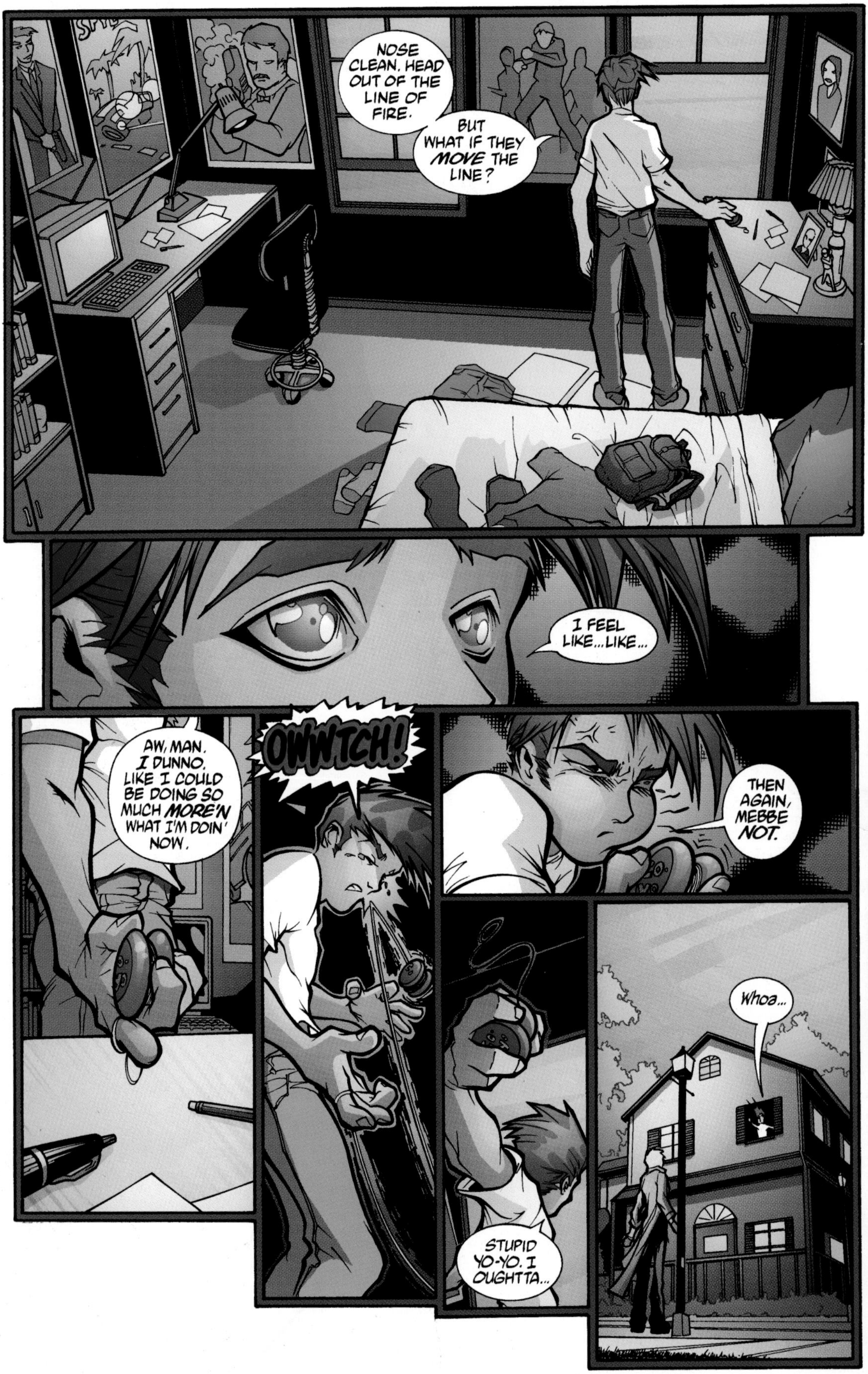
NOSE CLEAN. HEAD OUT OF THE LINE OF FIRE.
BUT WHAT IF THEY MOVE THE LINE?
I FEEL LIKE... LIKE...
AW, MAN. I DUNNO. LIKE I COULD BE DOING SO MUCH MORE'N WHAT I'M DOIN' NOW.
OWWTCH!
THEN AGAIN, MEBBE NOT.
STUPID YO-YO. I OUGHTTA...
Whoa...

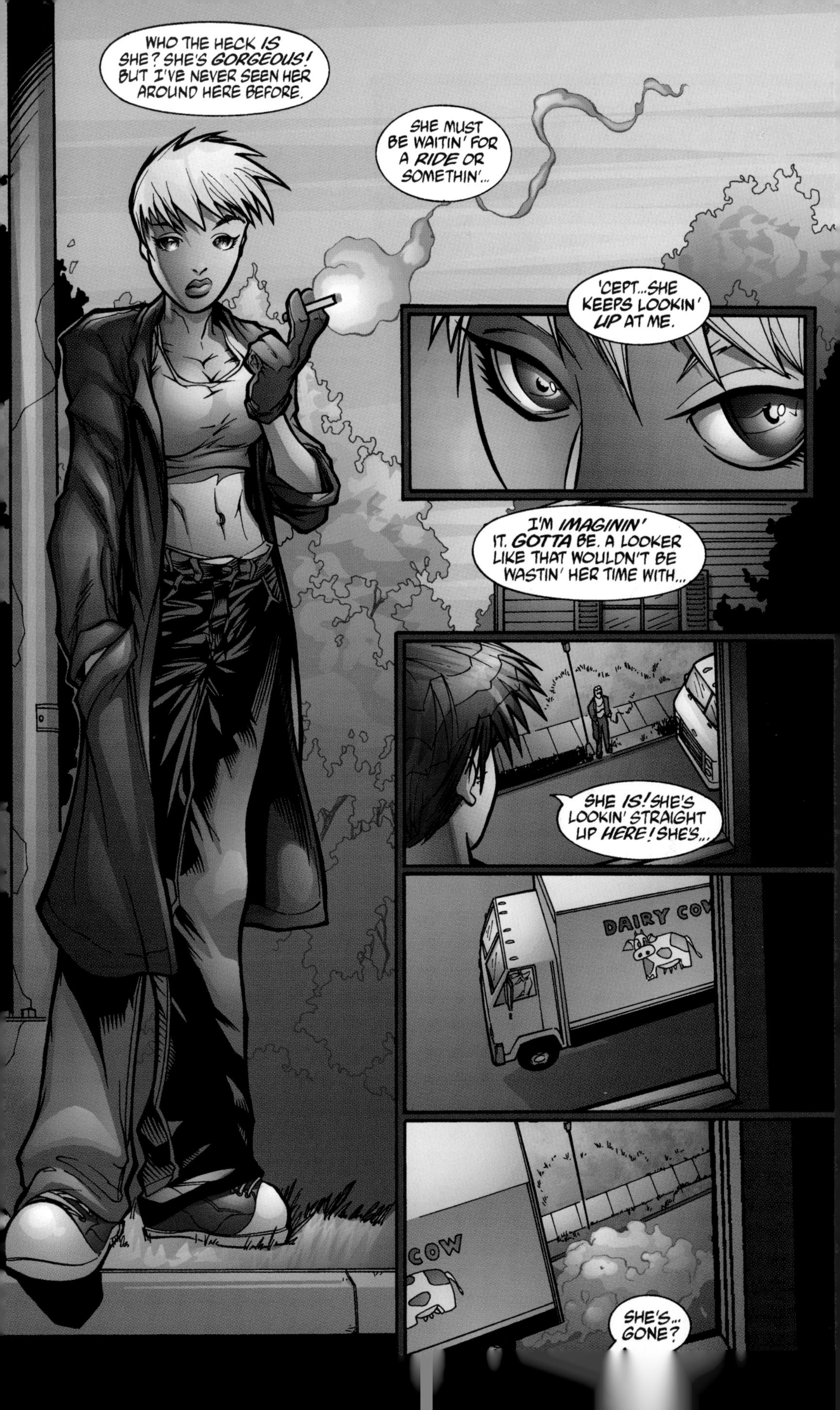
WHO THE HECK *IS* SHE? SHE'S *GORGEOUS!* BUT I'VE NEVER SEEN HER AROUND HERE BEFORE.
SHE MUST BE WAITIN' FOR A *RIDE* OR SOMETHIN'...
'CEPT...SHE KEEPS LOOKIN' *UP* AT ME.
I'M *IMAGININ'* IT. *GOTTA* BE. A LOOKER LIKE THAT WOULDN'T BE WASTIN' HER TIME WITH...
SHE *IS!* SHE'S LOOKIN' STRAIGHT UP *HERE!* SHE'S...
DAIRY COW
COW
SHE'S... GONE?

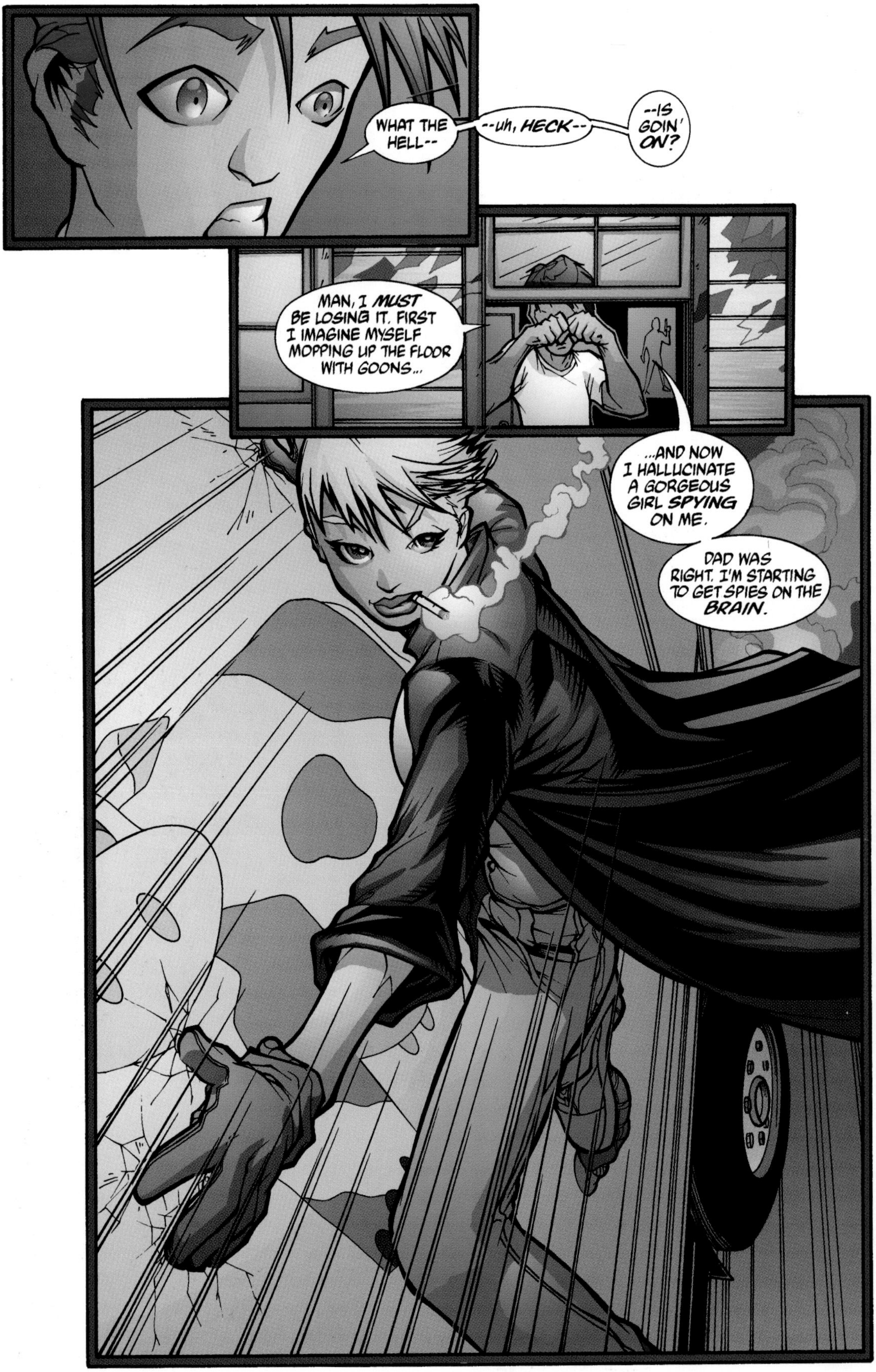
WHAT THE HELL--
--uh, HECK--
--IS GOIN' ON?
MAN, I MUST BE LOSING IT. FIRST I IMAGINE MYSELF MOPPING UP THE FLOOR WITH GOONS...
...AND NOW I HALLUCINATE A GORGEOUS GIRL SPYING ON ME.
DAD WAS RIGHT. I'M STARTING TO GET SPIES ON THE BRAIN.

TARGET ACQUIRED.

GET READY.

SAY, AFTER THIS, WE GRAB SOME *PIZZA* MAYBE?

I'M THERE... Uh-oh...I THINK SHE *MADE* US.

WHAT'S SHE *TOSSIN'*?

TIK TIK TIK TIK TIK TIK TIK

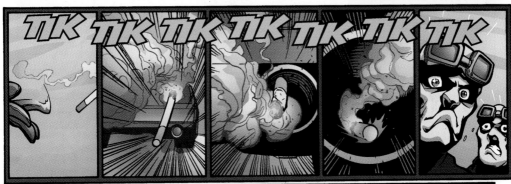

SAYONARA, S.K.I.N. HEADS...

COFFIN NAILS. THOSE THINGS'LL *KILL* YA.

"...WHILE TRAIN B LEAVES OHIO GOING 47 MILES..."

BOOOM

OH, WHO CARES. LET 'EM JUST *COLLIDE* AND GO--

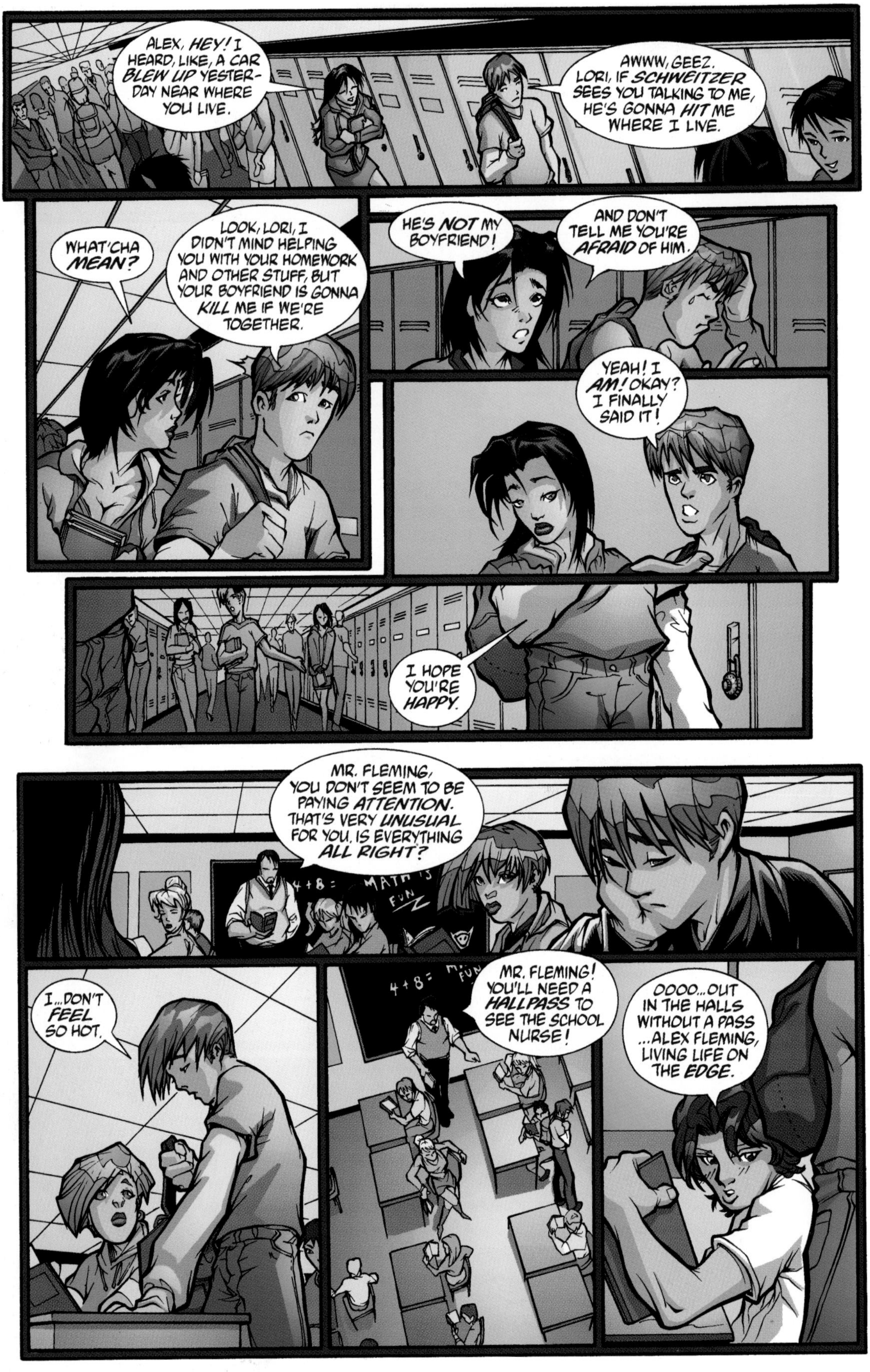

ALEX, HEY! I HEARD, LIKE, A CAR BLEW UP YESTERDAY NEAR WHERE YOU LIVE.
AWWW, GEEZ. LORI, IF SCHWEITZER SEES YOU TALKING TO ME, HE'S GONNA HIT ME WHERE I LIVE.
WHAT'CHA MEAN?
LOOK, LORI, I DIDN'T MIND HELPING YOU WITH YOUR HOMEWORK AND OTHER STUFF, BUT YOUR BOYFRIEND IS GONNA KILL ME IF WE'RE TOGETHER.
HE'S NOT MY BOYFRIEND!
AND DON'T TELL ME YOU'RE AFRAID OF HIM.
YEAH! I AM! OKAY? I FINALLY SAID IT!
I HOPE YOU'RE HAPPY.
MR. FLEMING, YOU DON'T SEEM TO BE PAYING ATTENTION. THAT'S VERY UNUSUAL FOR YOU. IS EVERYTHING ALL RIGHT?
4+8= MATH'S FUN
I...DON'T FEEL SO HOT.
MR. FLEMING! YOU'LL NEED A HALLPASS TO SEE THE SCHOOL NURSE!
OOOO...OUT IN THE HALLS WITHOUT A PASS ...ALEX FLEMING, LIVING LIFE ON THE EDGE.

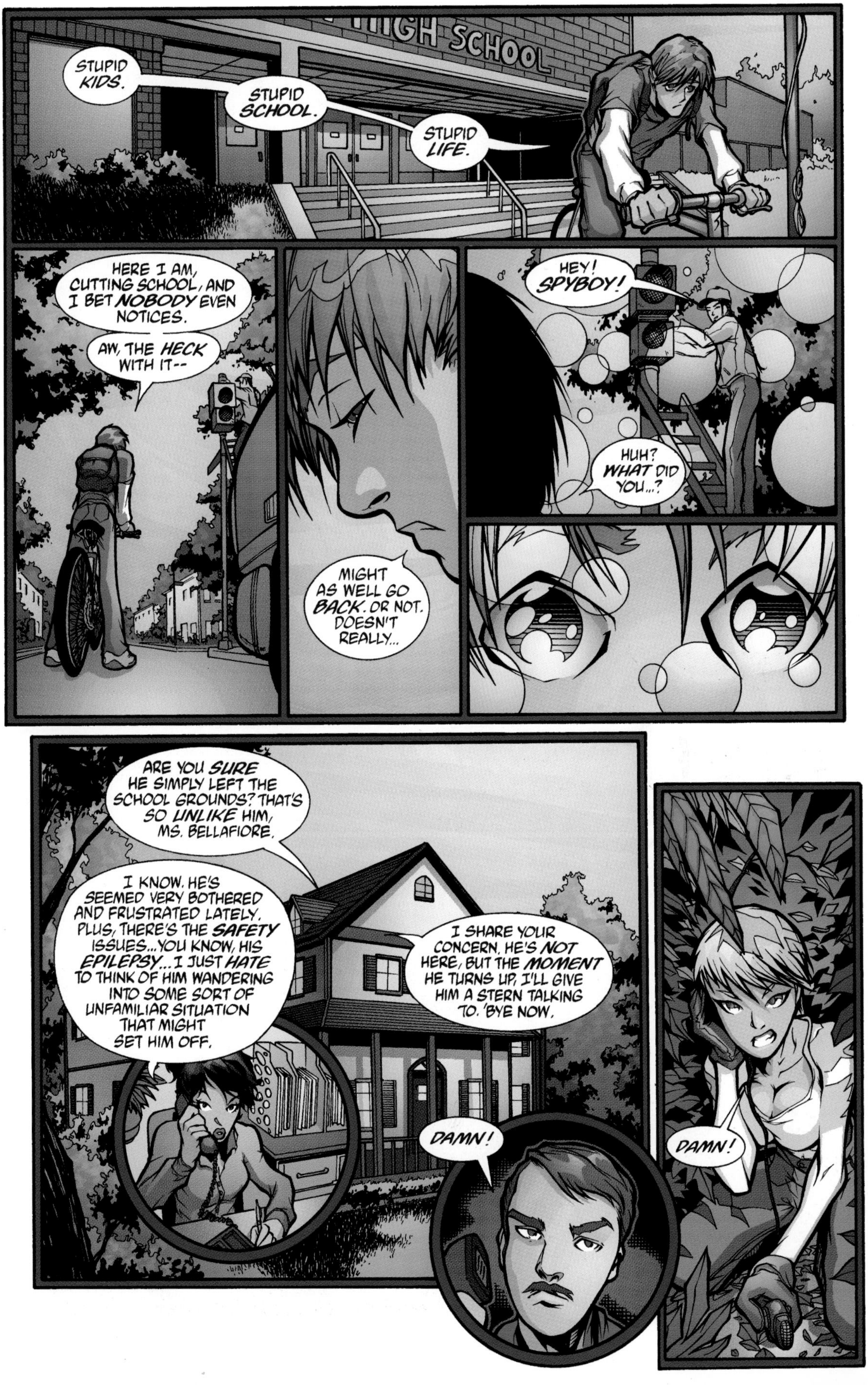
HIGH SCHOOL
STUPID KIDS.
STUPID SCHOOL.
STUPID LIFE.
HERE I AM, CUTTING SCHOOL, AND I BET NOBODY EVEN NOTICES.
AW, THE HECK WITH IT--
MIGHT AS WELL GO BACK. OR NOT. DOESN'T REALLY...
HEY! SPYBOY!
HUH? WHAT DID YOU...?
ARE YOU SURE HE SIMPLY LEFT THE SCHOOL GROUNDS? THAT'S SO UNLIKE HIM, MS. BELLAFIORE.
I KNOW. HE'S SEEMED VERY BOTHERED AND FRUSTRATED LATELY. PLUS, THERE'S THE SAFETY ISSUES...YOU KNOW, HIS EPILEPSY...I JUST HATE TO THINK OF HIM WANDERING INTO SOME SORT OF UNFAMILIAR SITUATION THAT MIGHT SET HIM OFF.
I SHARE YOUR CONCERN. HE'S NOT HERE, BUT THE MOMENT HE TURNS UP, I'LL GIVE HIM A STERN TALKING TO. 'BYE NOW.
DAMN!
DAMN!

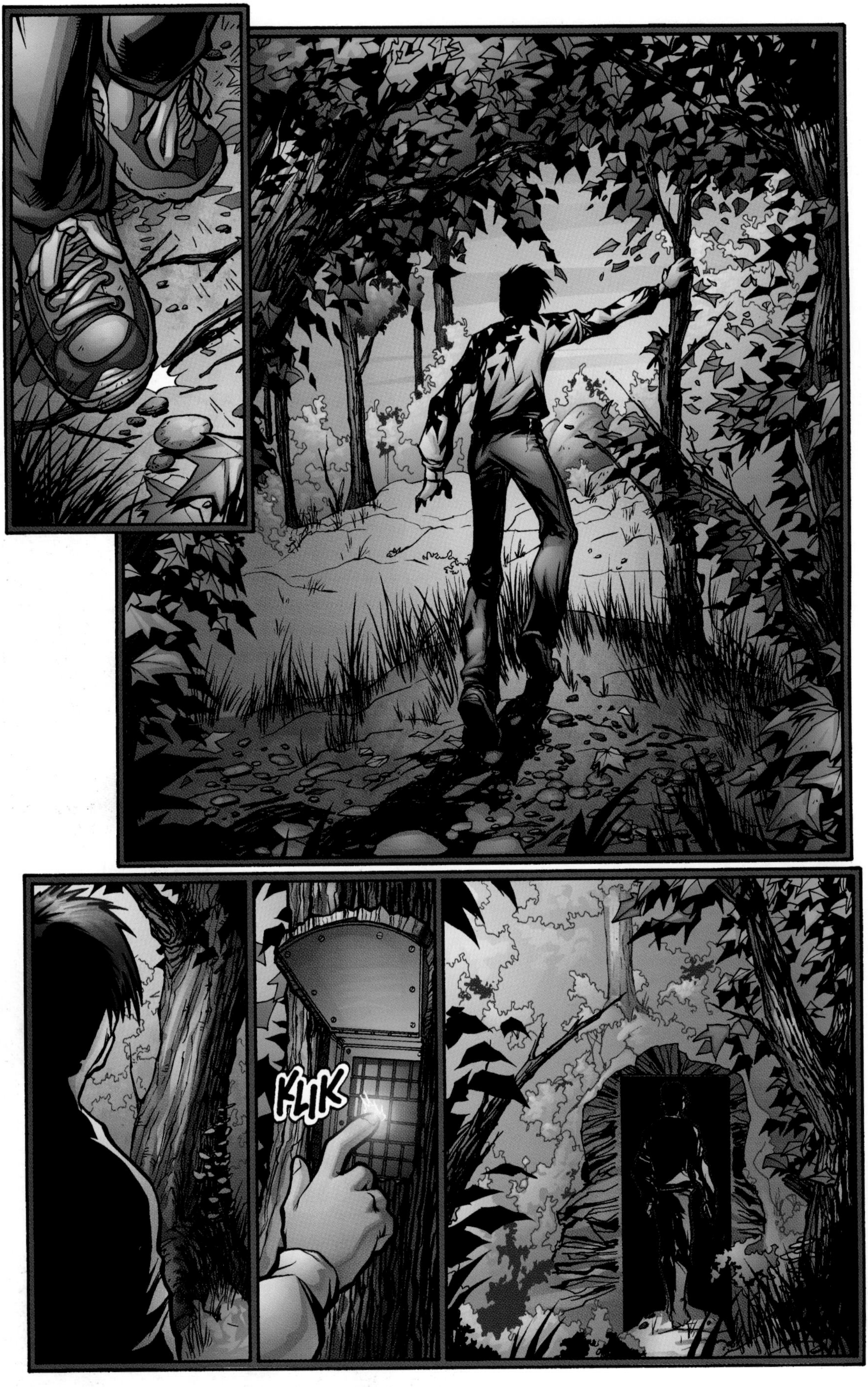
KLIK

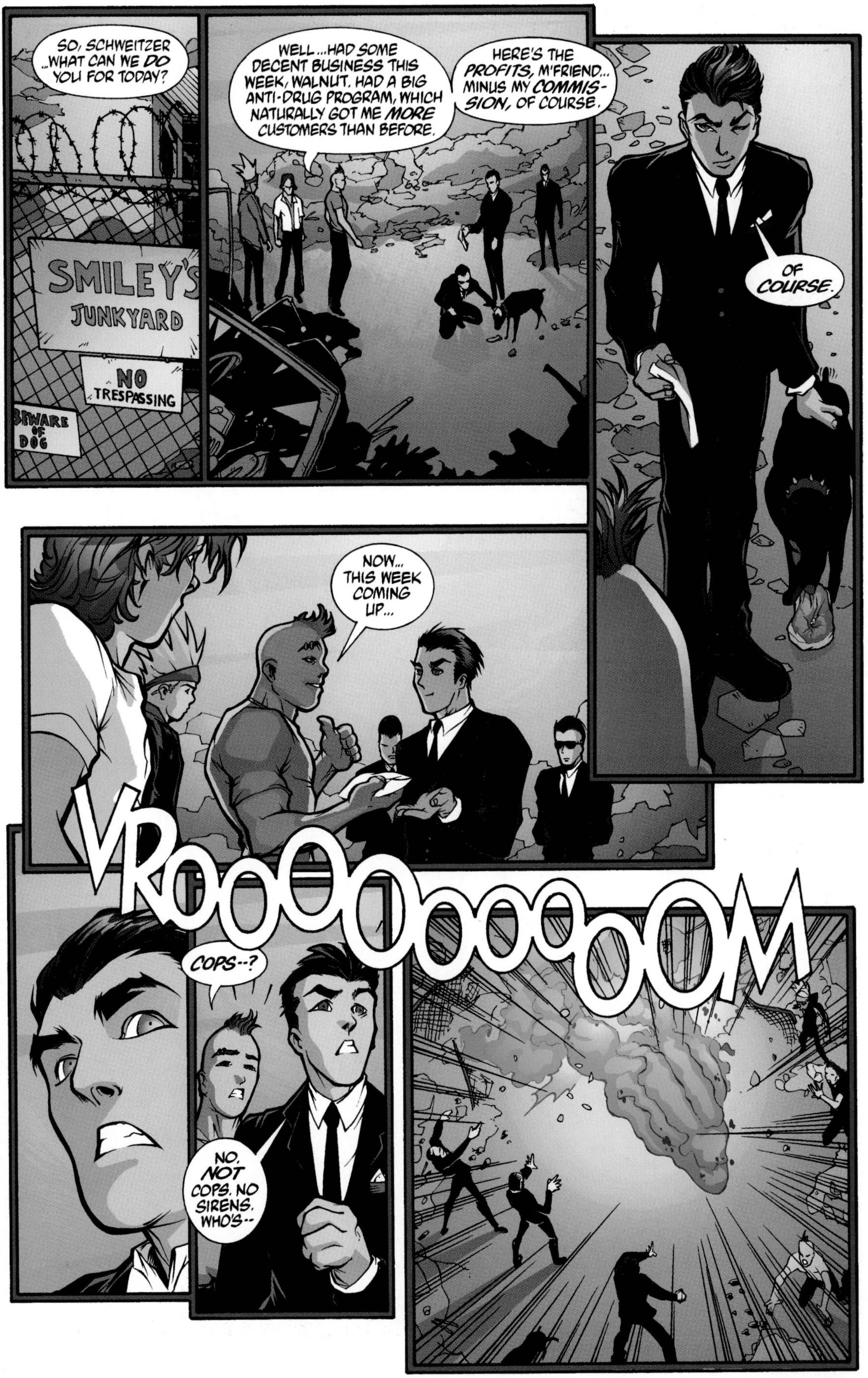
SO, SCHWEITZER ...WHAT CAN WE DO YOU FOR TODAY?
SMILEY'S JUNKYARD
NO TRESPASSING
BEWARE OF DOG
WELL ...HAD SOME DECENT BUSINESS THIS WEEK, WALNUT. HAD A BIG ANTI-DRUG PROGRAM, WHICH NATURALLY GOT ME MORE CUSTOMERS THAN BEFORE.
HERE'S THE PROFITS, M'FRIEND... MINUS MY COMMISSION, OF COURSE.
OF COURSE.
NOW... THIS WEEK COMING UP...
VROOOOOOOOOM
COPS--?
NO, NOT COPS. NO SIRENS. WHO'S--

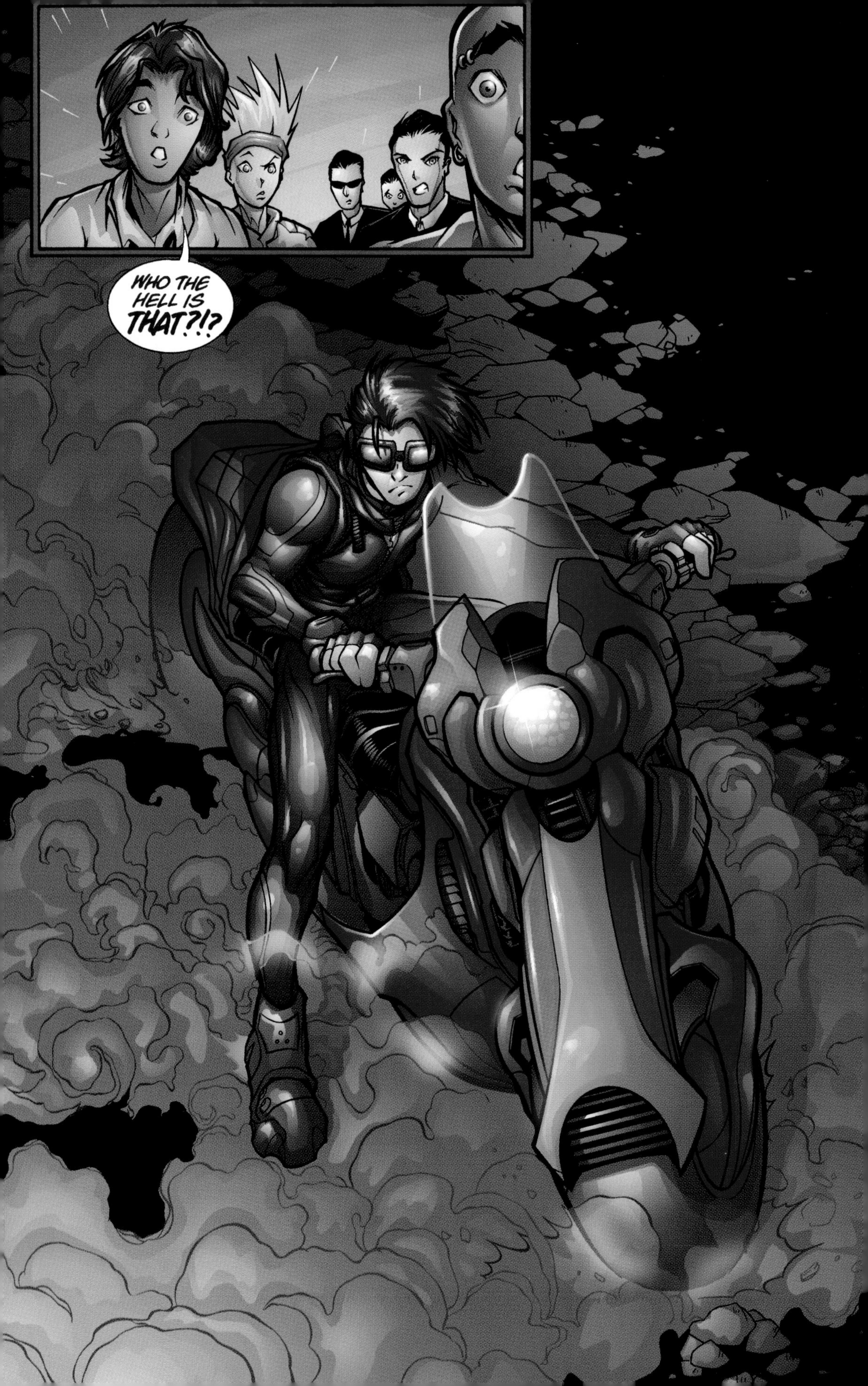
WHO THE HELL IS THAT?!?

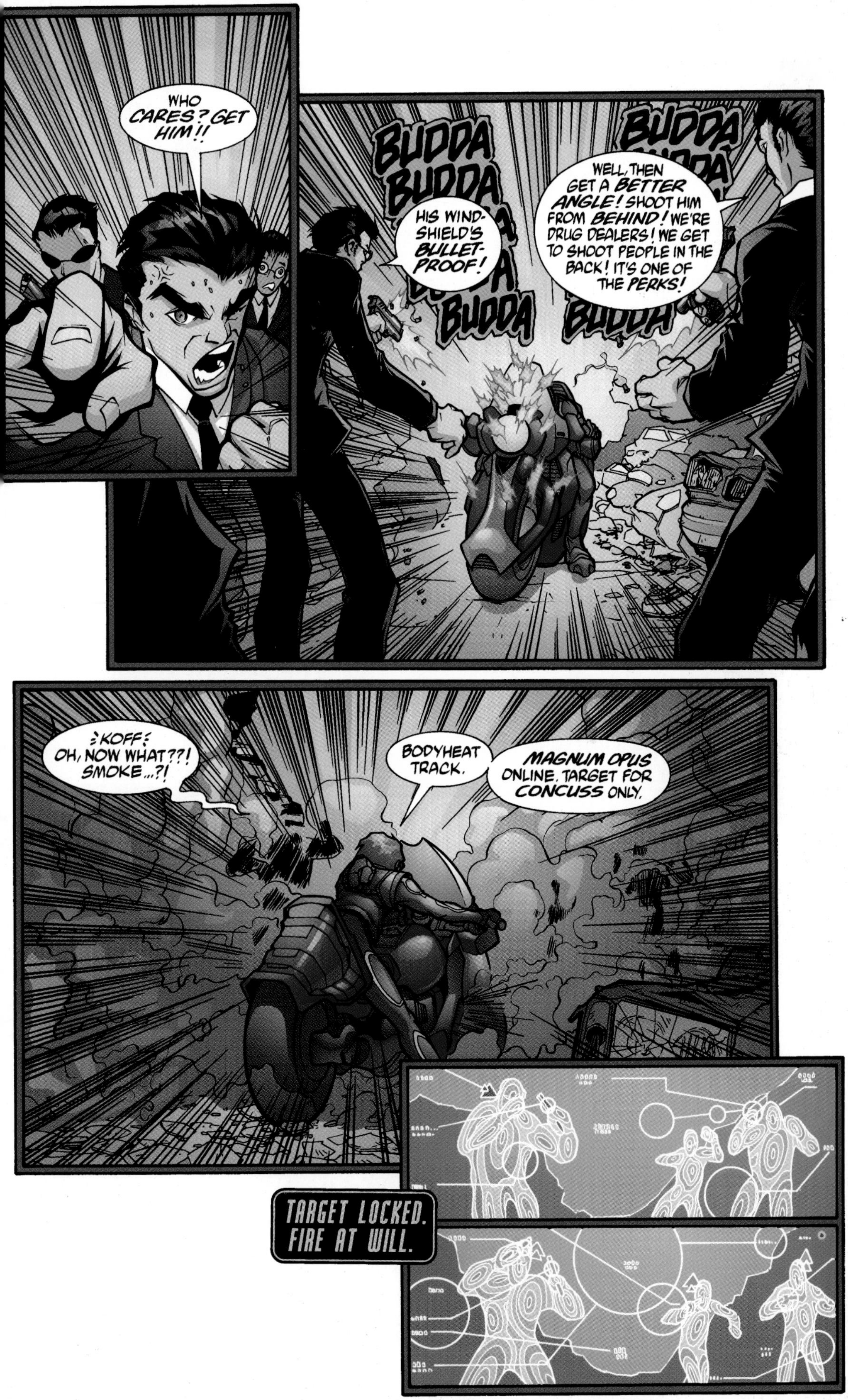

WHO CARES? GET HIM!!
BUDDA BUDDA
HIS WIND-SHIELD'S BULLET-PROOF!
BUDDA
WELL, THEN GET A BETTER ANGLE! SHOOT HIM FROM BEHIND! WE'RE DRUG DEALERS! WE GET TO SHOOT PEOPLE IN THE BACK! IT'S ONE OF THE PERKS!
BUDDA
≈KOFF≈ OH, NOW WHAT??! SMOKE...?!
BODYHEAT TRACK.
MAGNUM OPUS ONLINE. TARGET FOR CONCUSS ONLY.
TARGET LOCKED. FIRE AT WILL.

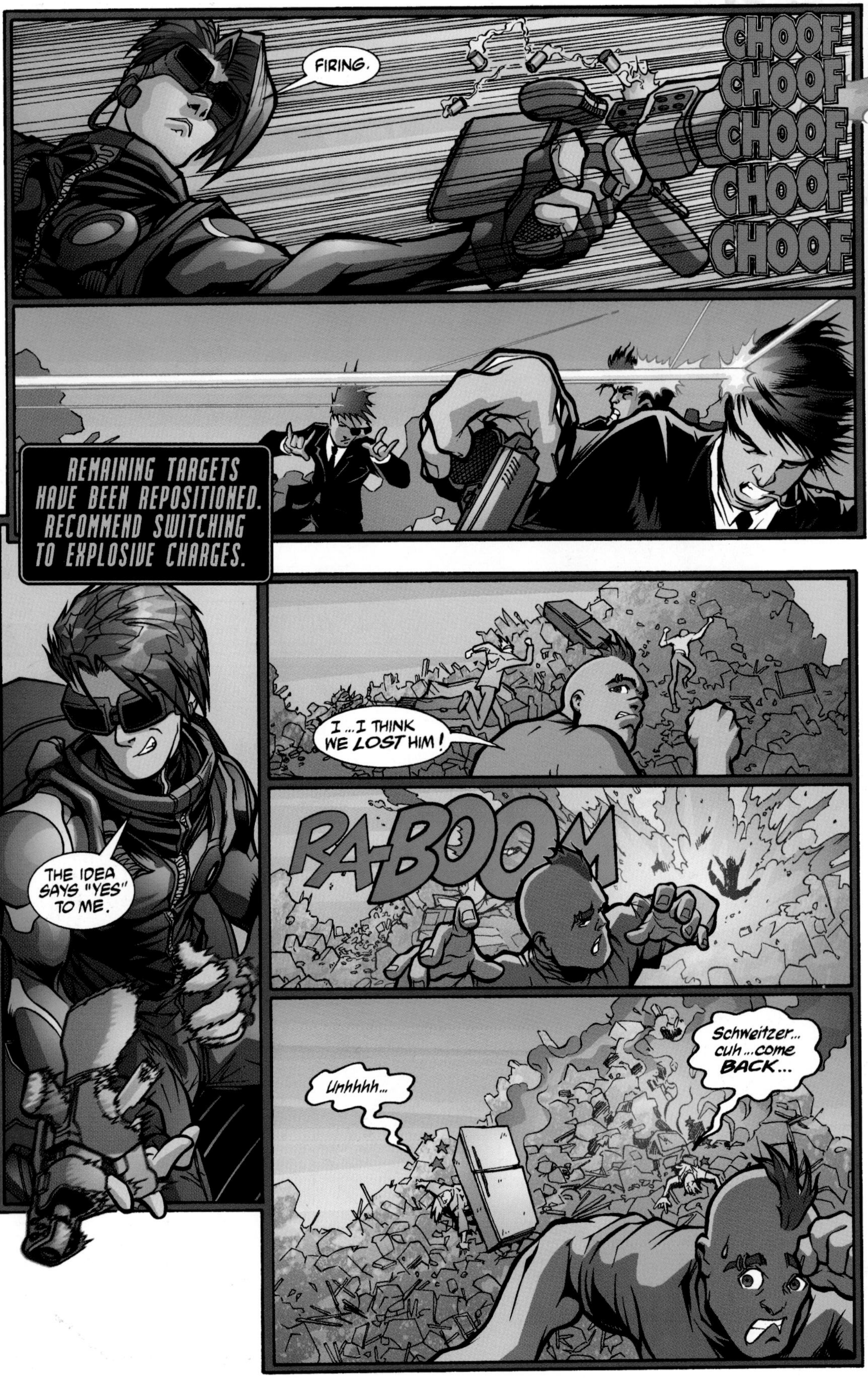
FIRING.
CHOOF CHOOF CHOOF CHOOF CHOOF
REMAINING TARGETS HAVE BEEN REPOSITIONED. RECOMMEND SWITCHING TO EXPLOSIVE CHARGES.
THE IDEA SAYS "YES" TO ME.
I...I THINK WE LOST HIM!
RA-BOOM
Unhhhh...
Schweitzer... cuh...come BACK...

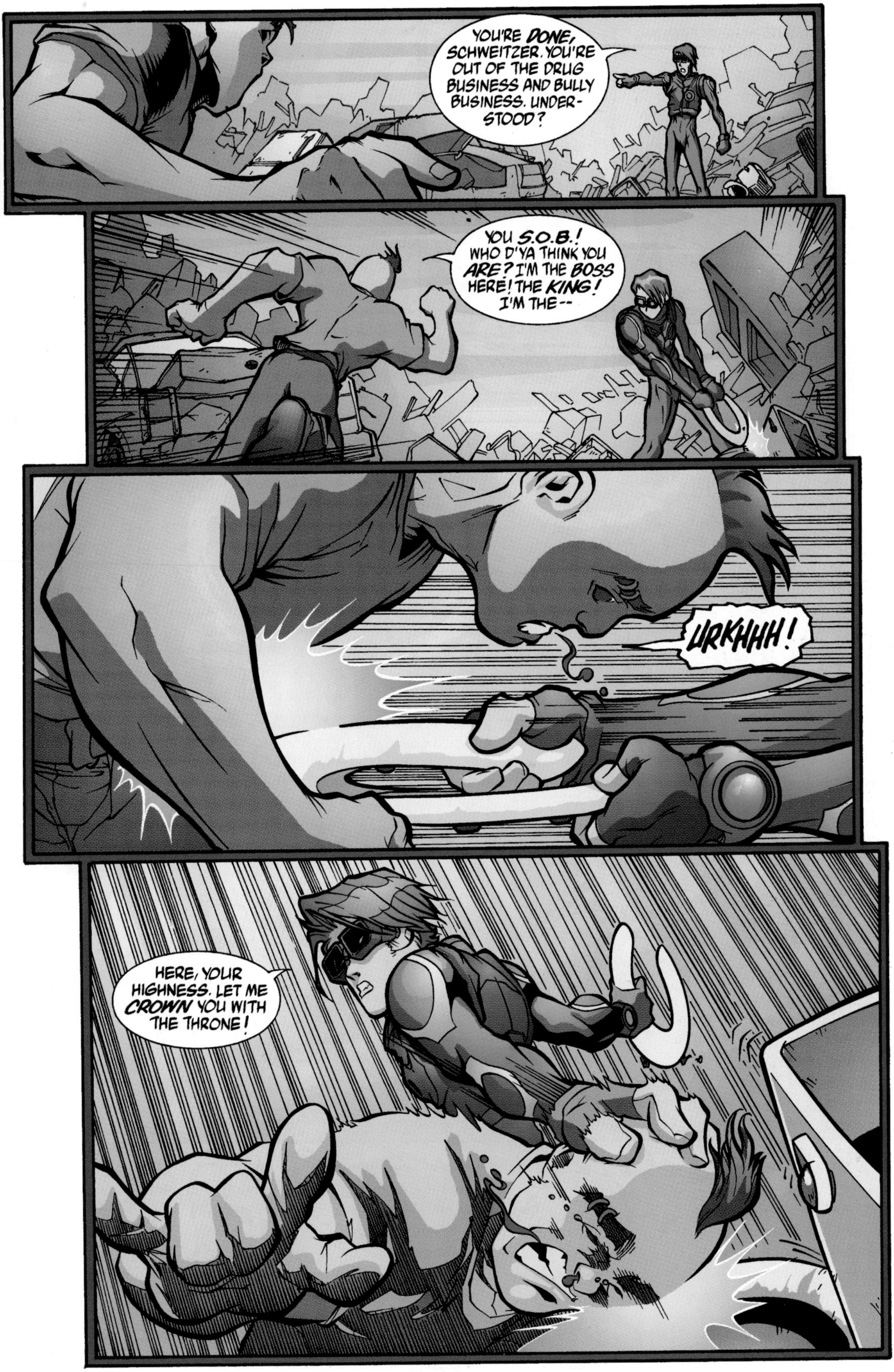
YOU'RE DONE, SCHWEITZER. YOU'RE OUT OF THE DRUG BUSINESS AND BULLY BUSINESS. UNDER-STOOD?
YOU S.O.B.! WHO D'YA THINK YOU ARE? I'M THE BOSS HERE! THE KING! I'M THE--
URKHHH!
HERE, YOUR HIGHNESS. LET ME CROWN YOU WITH THE THRONE!

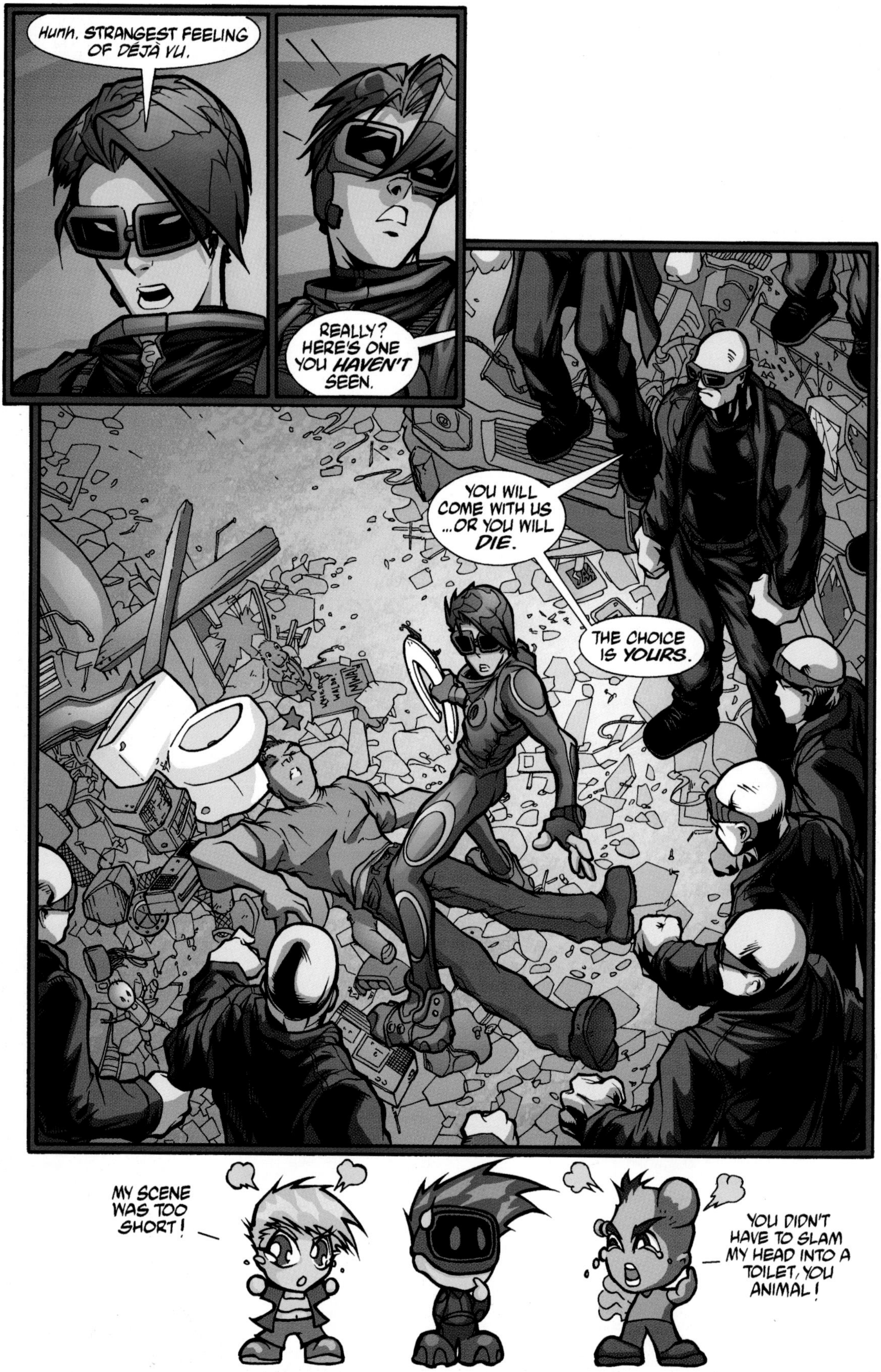
Hunh. STRANGEST FEELING OF DÉJÀ VU.
REALLY? HERE'S ONE YOU HAVEN'T SEEN.
YOU WILL COME WITH US ...OR YOU WILL DIE.
THE CHOICE IS YOURS.
MY SCENE WAS TOO SHORT!
YOU DIDN'T HAVE TO SLAM MY HEAD INTO A TOILET, YOU ANIMAL!

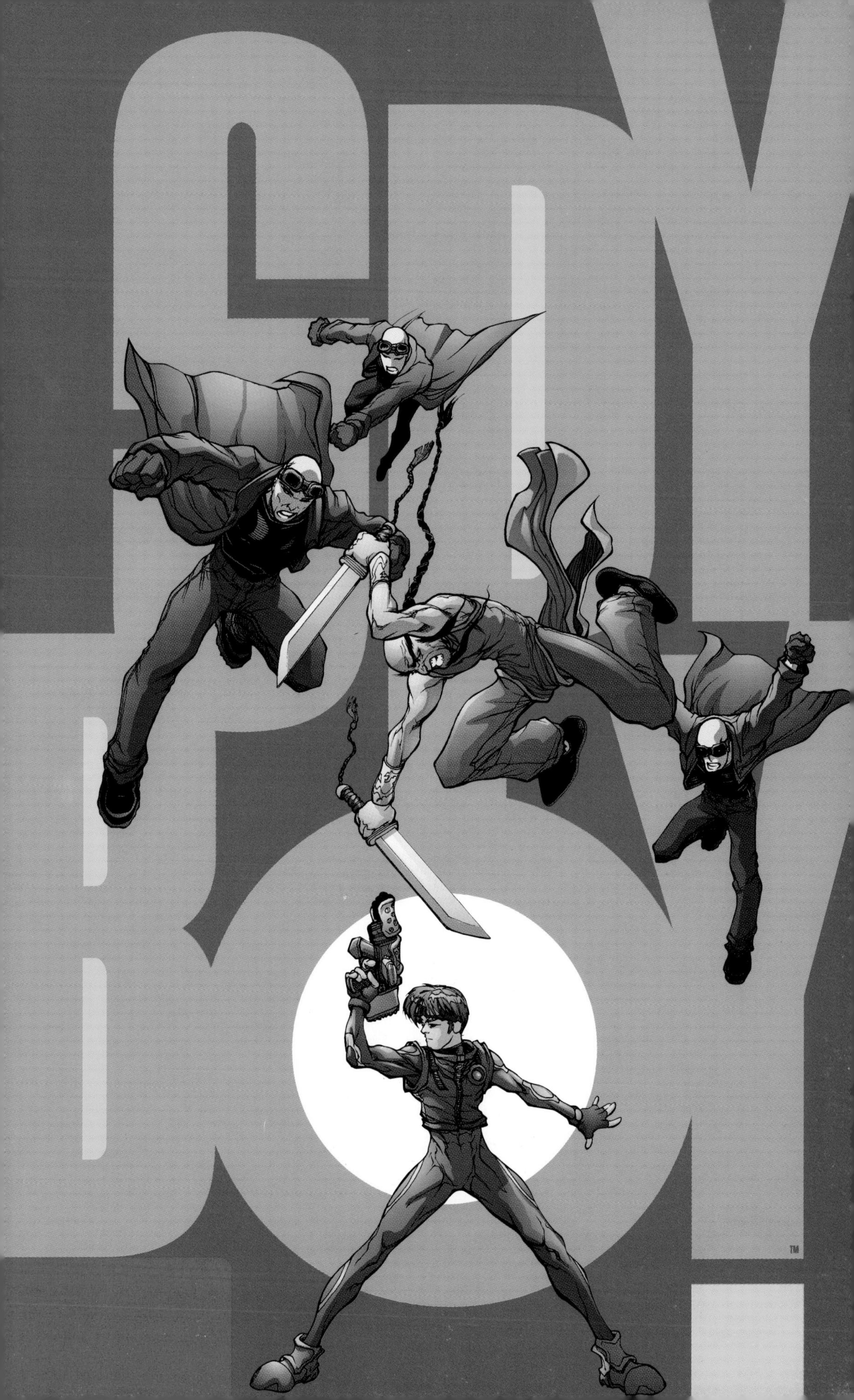
SPYBOY!
TM

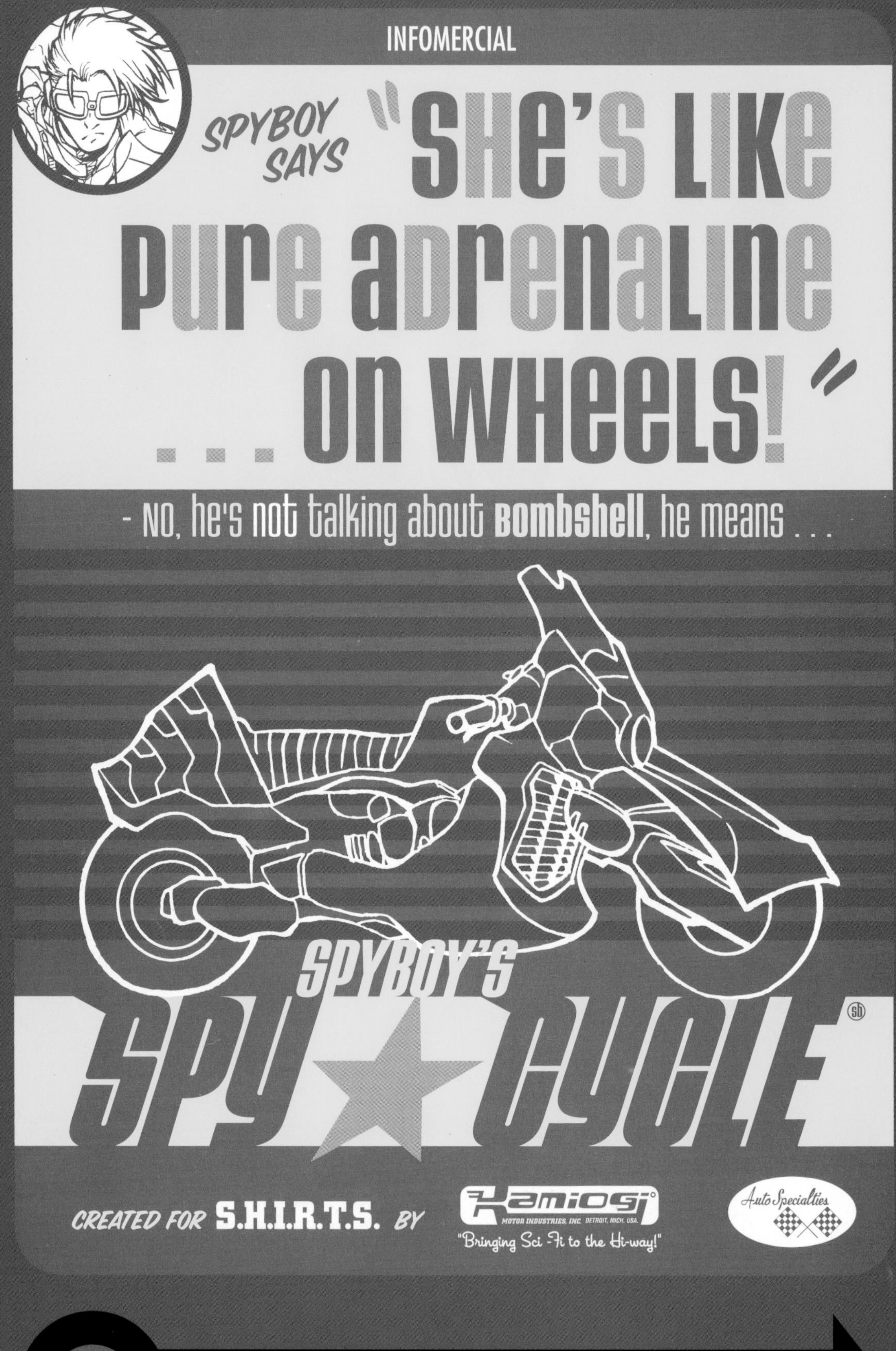
INFOMERCIAL
SPYBOY SAYS
"SHE'S LIKE PURE ADRENALINE ...ON WHEELS!"
- NO, he's not talking about Bombshell, he means . . .
SPYBOY'S
SPY★CYCLE
CREATED FOR S.H.I.R.T.S. BY
Kamiogi MOTOR INDUSTRIES, INC. DETROIT, MICH. USA.
"Bringing Sci-Fi to the Hi-way!"
Auto Specialties

2 "LIVE AND LET FRY"

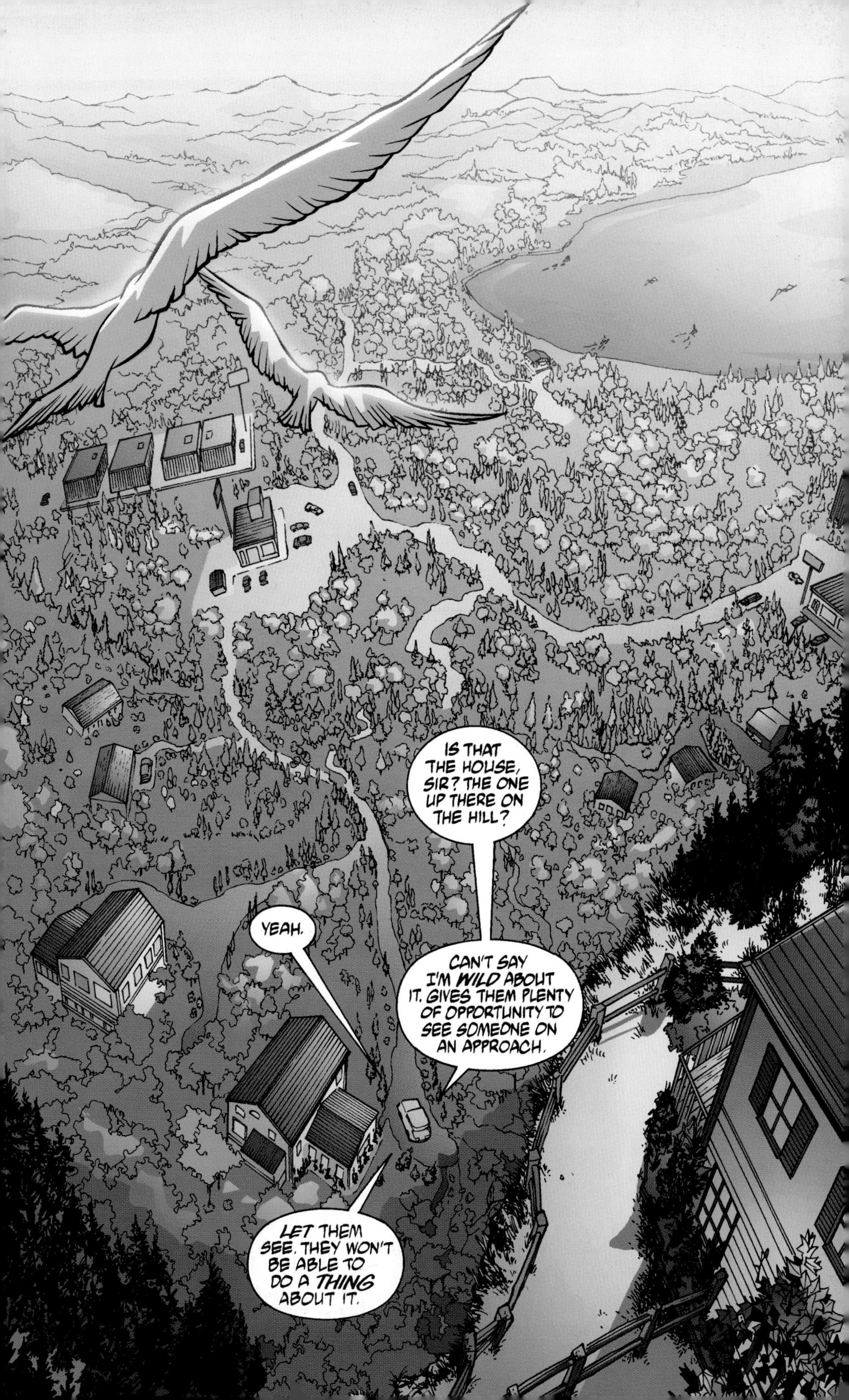
IS THAT THE HOUSE, SIR? THE ONE UP THERE ON THE HILL?
YEAH.
CAN'T SAY I'M *WILD* ABOUT IT. GIVES THEM PLENTY OF OPPORTUNITY TO SEE SOMEONE ON AN APPROACH.
LET THEM SEE. THEY WON'T BE ABLE TO DO A *THING* ABOUT IT.

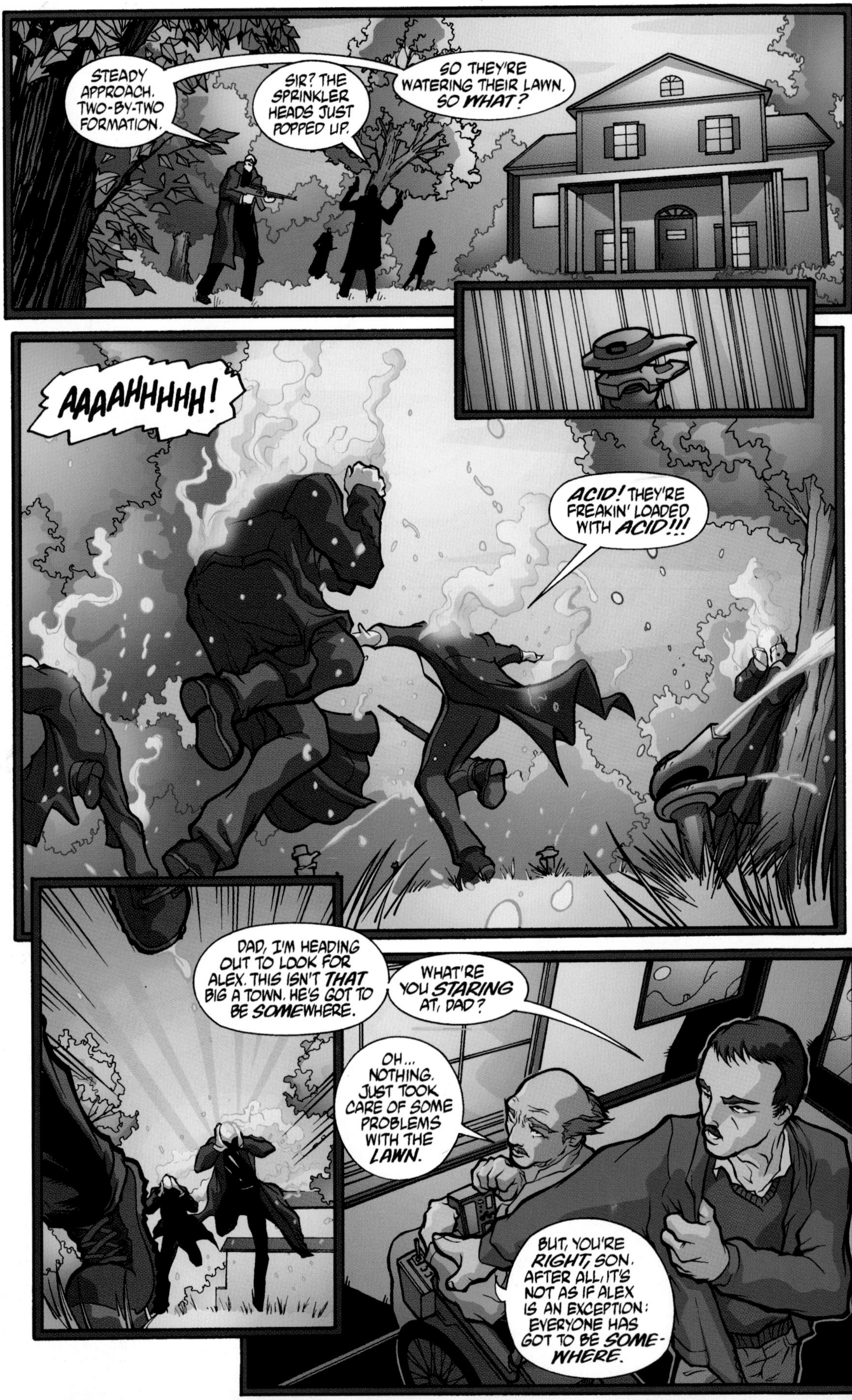
STEADY APPROACH. TWO-BY-TWO FORMATION.
SIR? THE SPRINKLER HEADS JUST POPPED UP.
SO THEY'RE WATERING THEIR LAWN. SO WHAT?
AAAAHHHHH!
ACID! THEY'RE FREAKIN' LOADED WITH ACID!!!
DAD, I'M HEADING OUT TO LOOK FOR ALEX. THIS ISN'T THAT BIG A TOWN. HE'S GOT TO BE SOMEWHERE.
WHAT'RE YOU STARING AT, DAD?
OH... NOTHING. JUST TOOK CARE OF SOME PROBLEMS WITH THE LAWN.
BUT, YOU'RE RIGHT, SON. AFTER ALL, IT'S NOT AS IF ALEX IS AN EXCEPTION: EVERYONE HAS GOT TO BE SOME-WHERE.

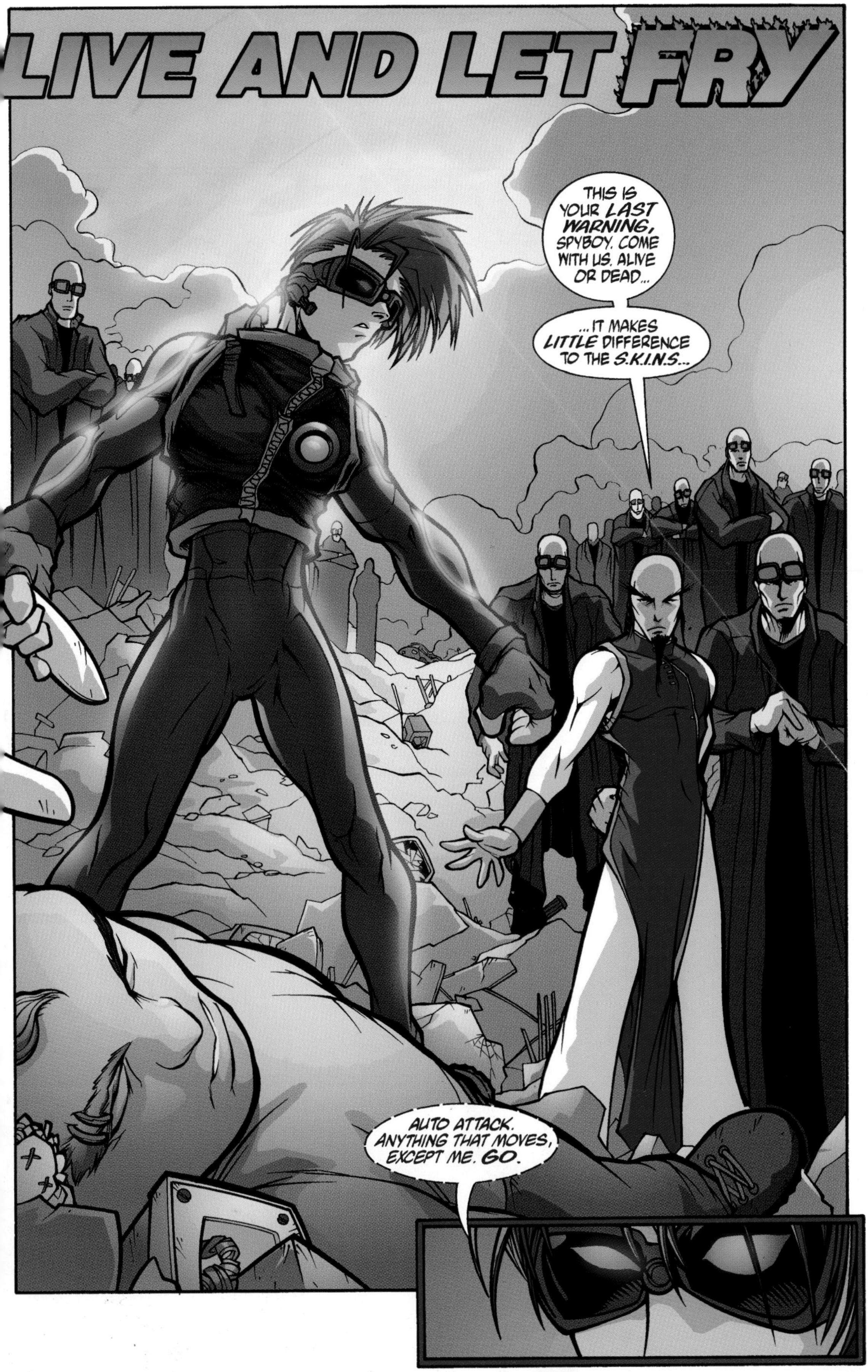

LIVE AND LET FRY
THIS IS YOUR LAST WARNING, SPYBOY. COME WITH US. ALIVE OR DEAD...
...IT MAKES LITTLE DIFFERENCE TO THE S.K.I.N.S...
AUTO ATTACK. ANYTHING THAT MOVES, EXCEPT ME. GO.

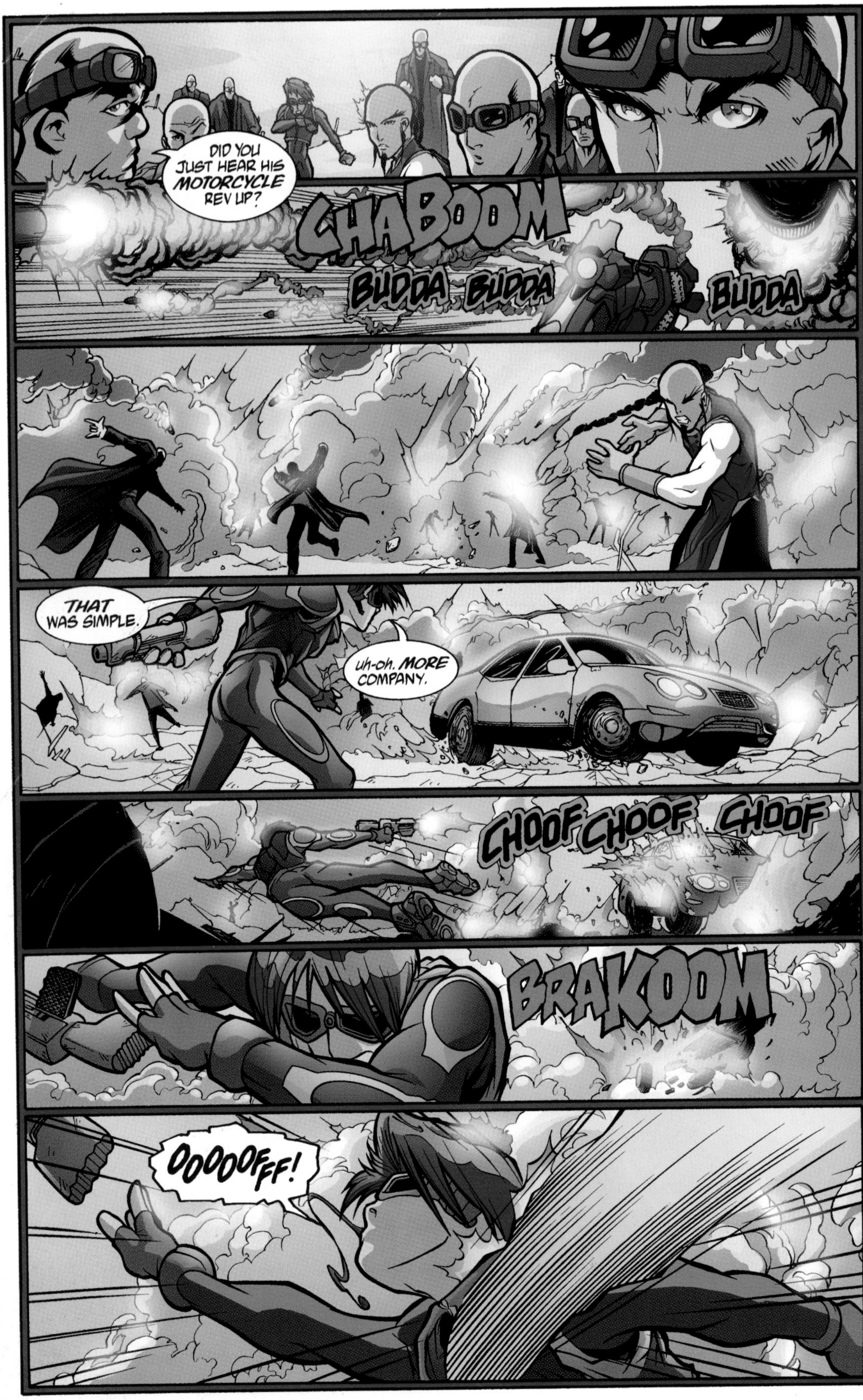
DID YOU JUST HEAR HIS MOTORCYCLE REV UP?
CHABOOM
BUDDA BUDDA
BUDDA
THAT WAS SIMPLE.
uh-oh. MORE COMPANY.
CHOOF CHOOF CHOOF
BRAKOOM
OOOOOFFF!

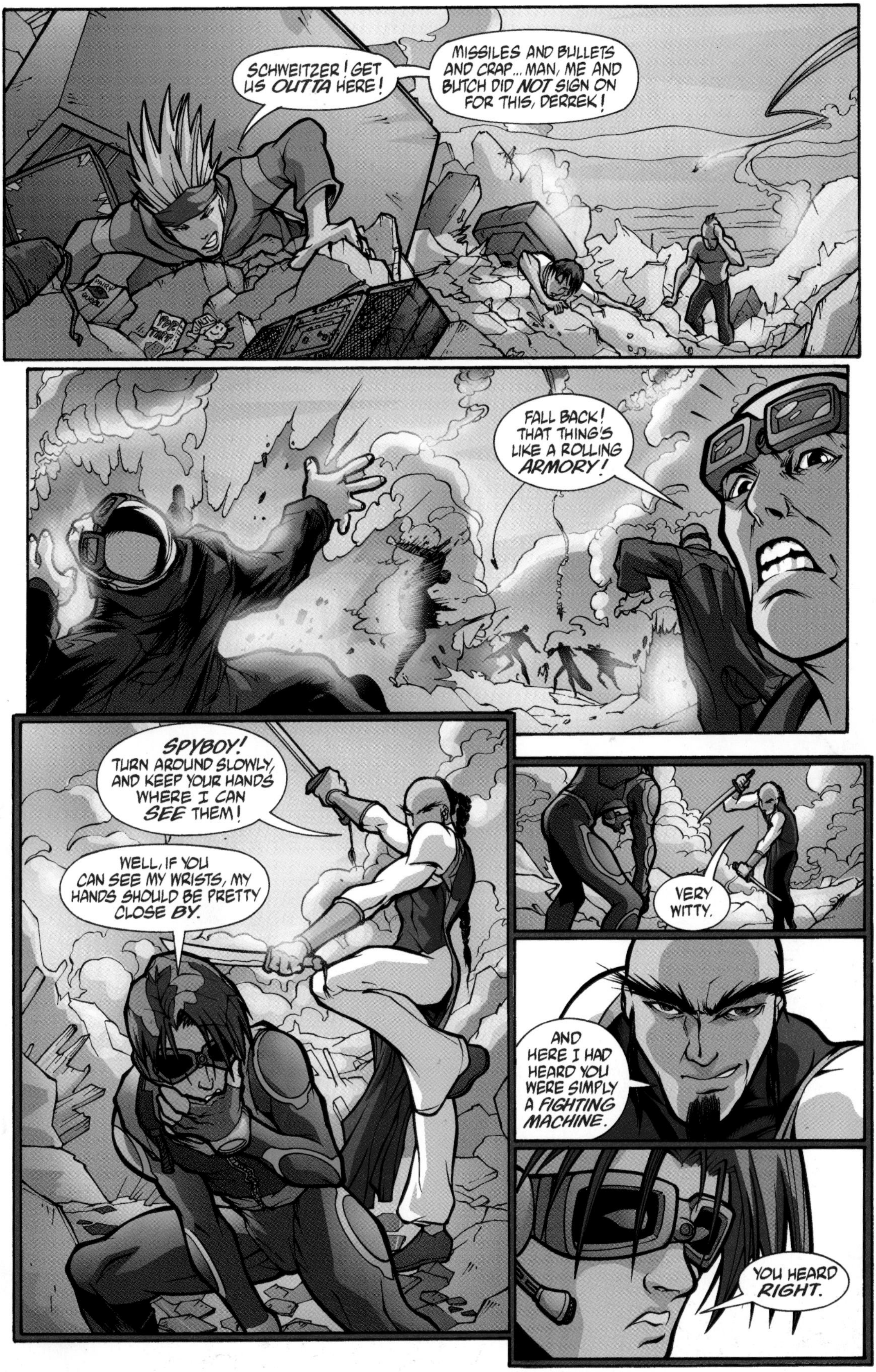
SCHWEITZER! GET US OUTTA HERE!
MISSILES AND BULLETS AND CRAP... MAN, ME AND BUTCH DID NOT SIGN ON FOR THIS, DERREK!
FALL BACK! THAT THING'S LIKE A ROLLING ARMORY!
SPYBOY! TURN AROUND SLOWLY, AND KEEP YOUR HANDS WHERE I CAN SEE THEM!
WELL, IF YOU CAN SEE MY WRISTS, MY HANDS SHOULD BE PRETTY CLOSE BY.
VERY WITTY.
AND HERE I HAD HEARD YOU WERE SIMPLY A FIGHTING MACHINE.
YOU HEARD RIGHT.

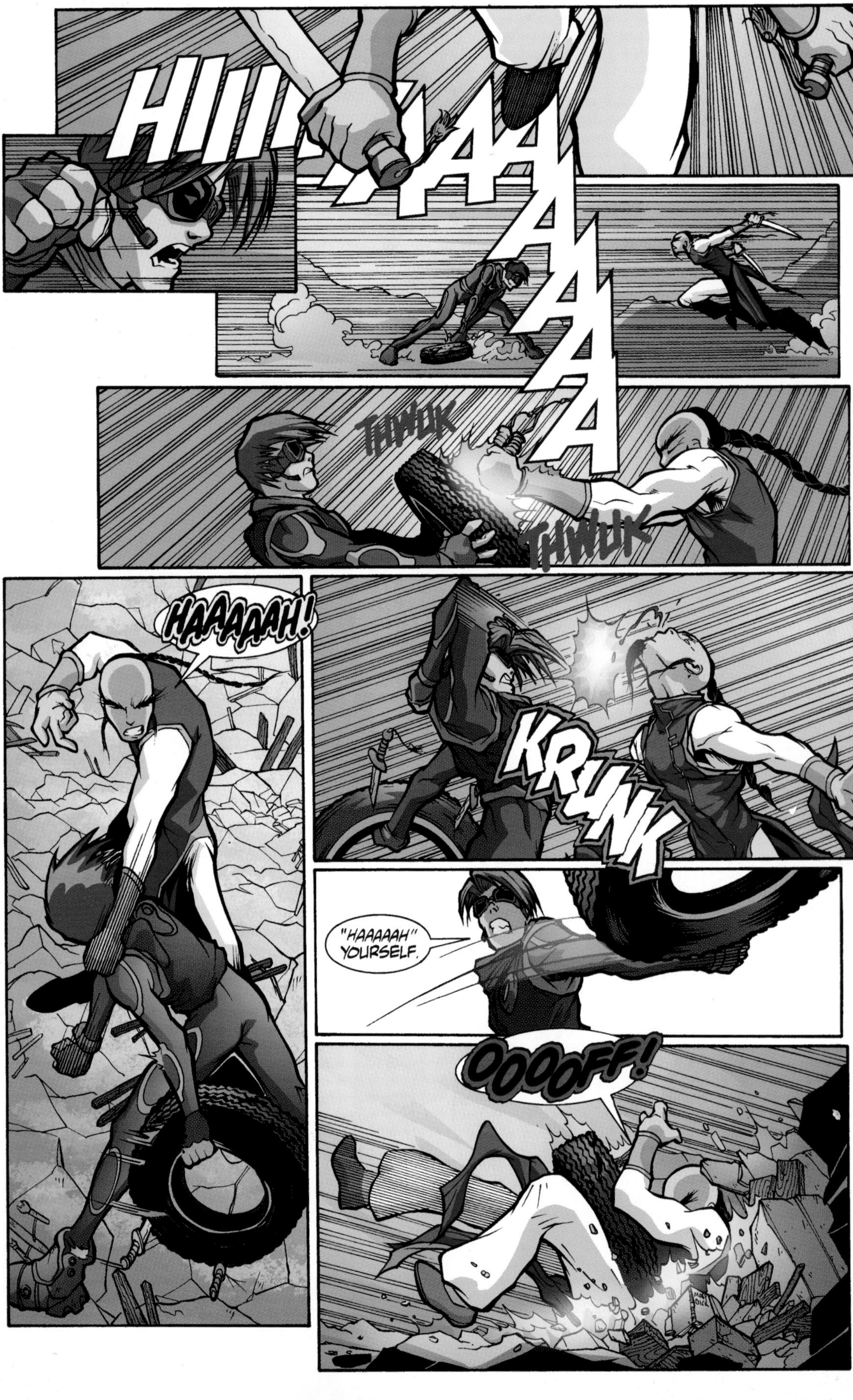
HIIIYAAAAAAAAA
THWUK
THWUK
HAAAAAH!
KRUNK
"HAAAAAH" YOURSELF.
OOOOOFF!

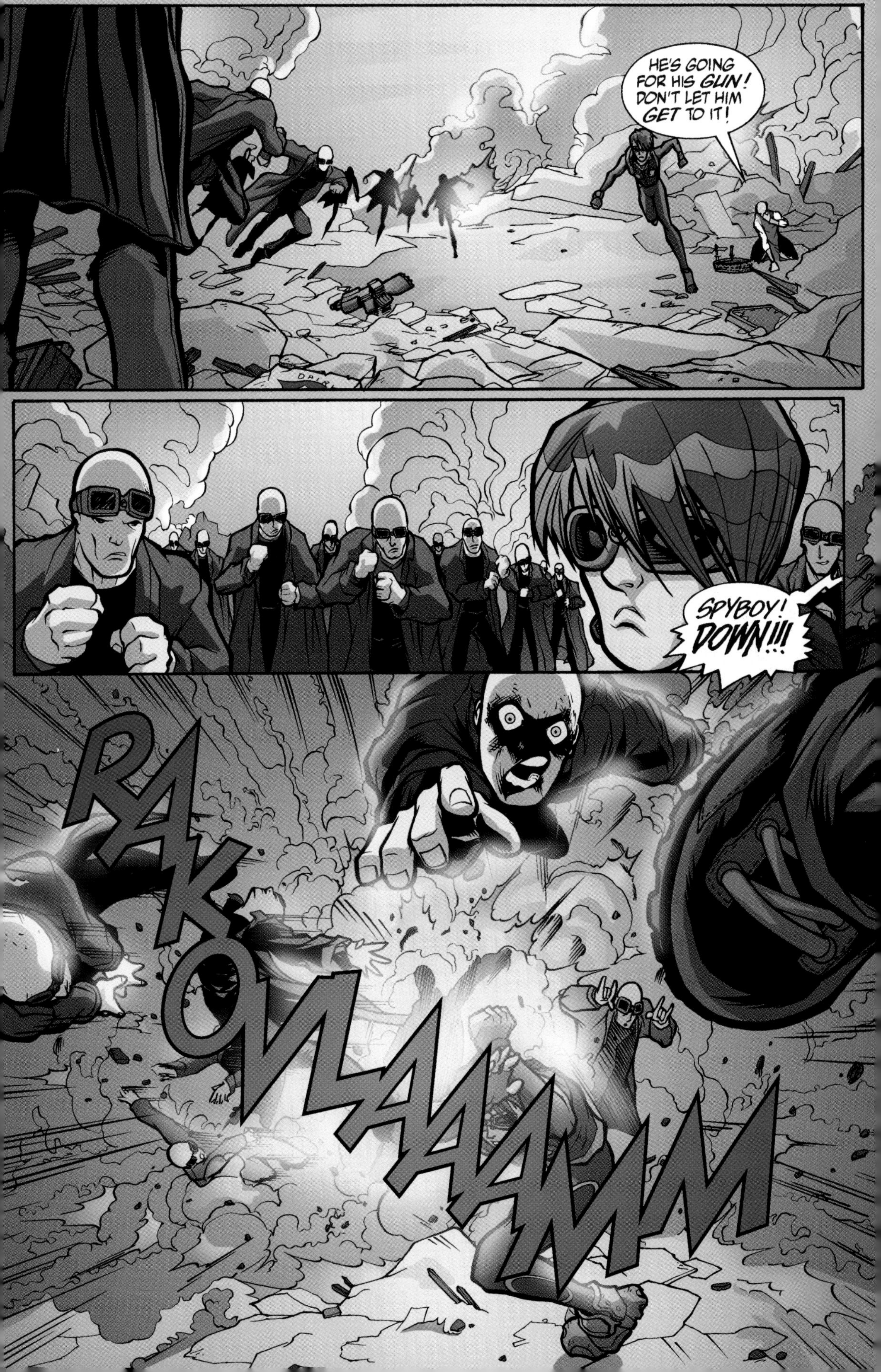
HE'S GOING FOR HIS GUN! DON'T LET HIM GET TO IT!
SPYBOY! DOWN!!!
RAKOWAAAMM

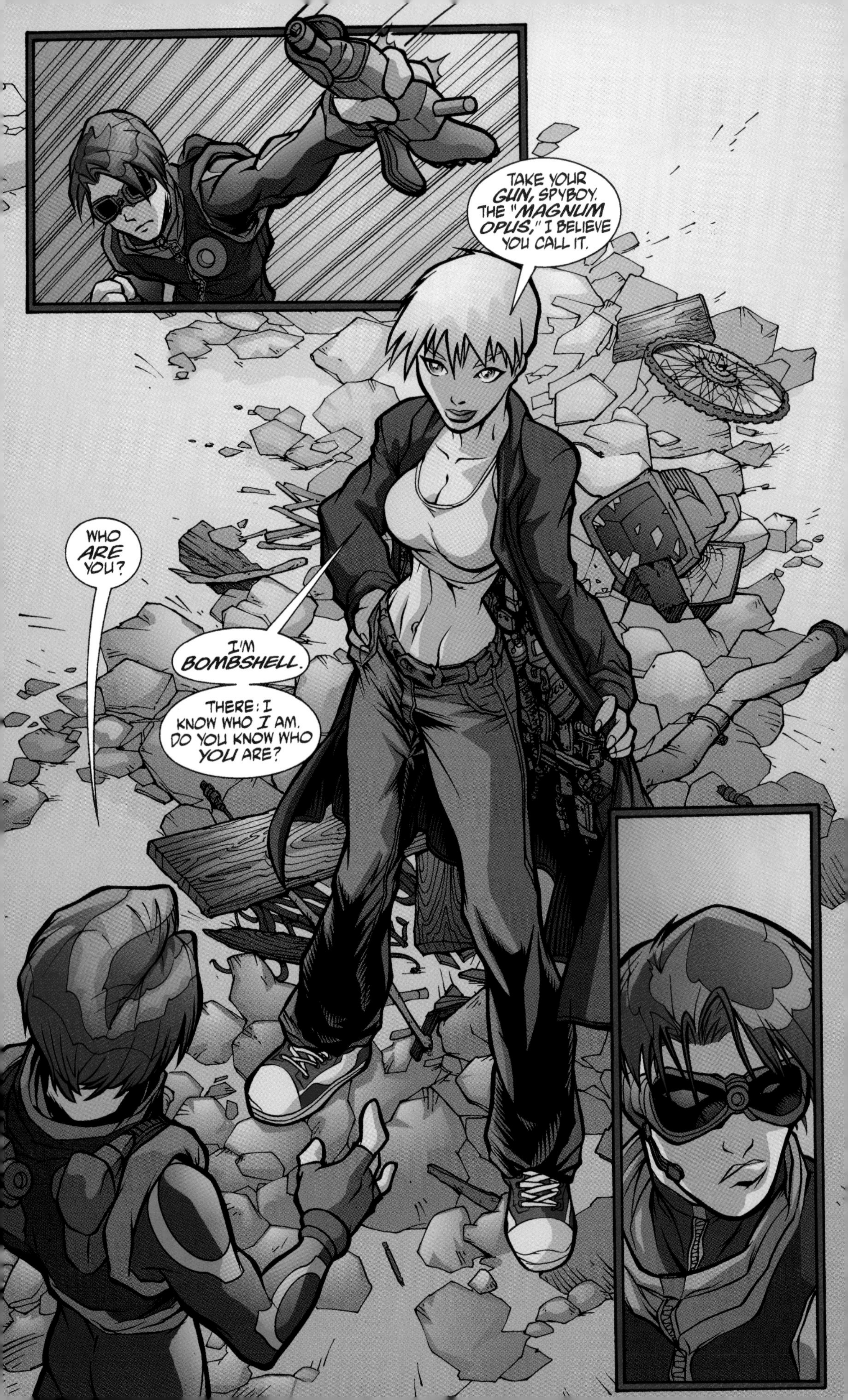
TAKE YOUR GUN, SPYBOY. THE "MAGNUM OPUS," I BELIEVE YOU CALL IT.
WHO ARE YOU?
I'M BOMBSHELL.
THERE: I KNOW WHO I AM. DO YOU KNOW WHO YOU ARE?

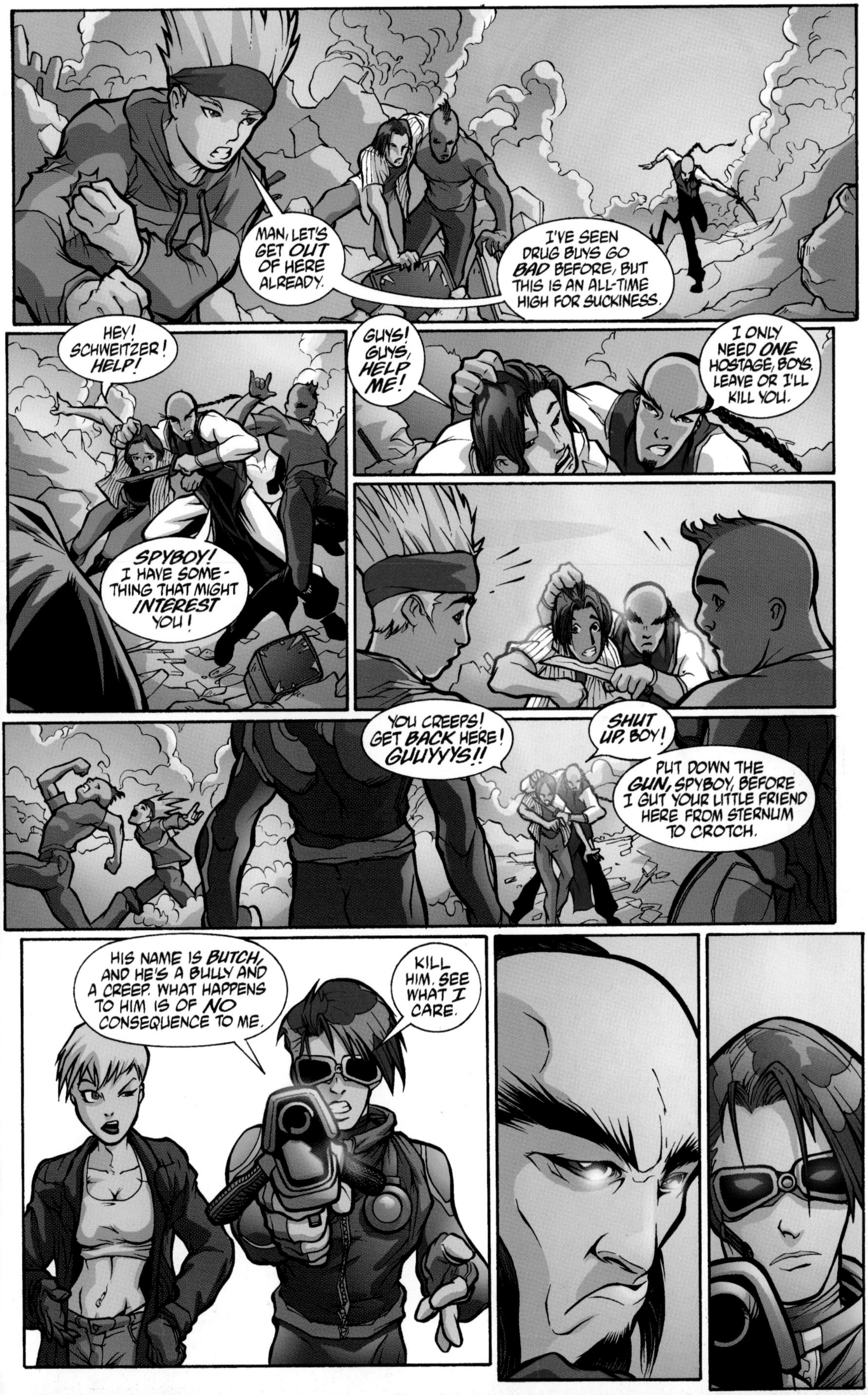
MAN, LET'S GET OUT OF HERE ALREADY.
I'VE SEEN DRUG BUYS GO BAD BEFORE, BUT THIS IS AN ALL-TIME HIGH FOR SUCKINESS.
HEY! SCHWEITZER! HELP!
SPYBOY! I HAVE SOME-THING THAT MIGHT INTEREST YOU!
GUYS! GUYS, HELP ME!
I ONLY NEED ONE HOSTAGE, BOYS. LEAVE OR I'LL KILL YOU.
YOU CREEPS! GET BACK HERE! GUUYYYS!!
SHUT UP, BOY!
PUT DOWN THE GUN, SPYBOY, BEFORE I GUT YOUR LITTLE FRIEND HERE FROM STERNUM TO CROTCH.
HIS NAME IS BUTCH, AND HE'S A BULLY AND A CREEP. WHAT HAPPENS TO HIM IS OF NO CONSEQUENCE TO ME.
KILL HIM. SEE WHAT I CARE.

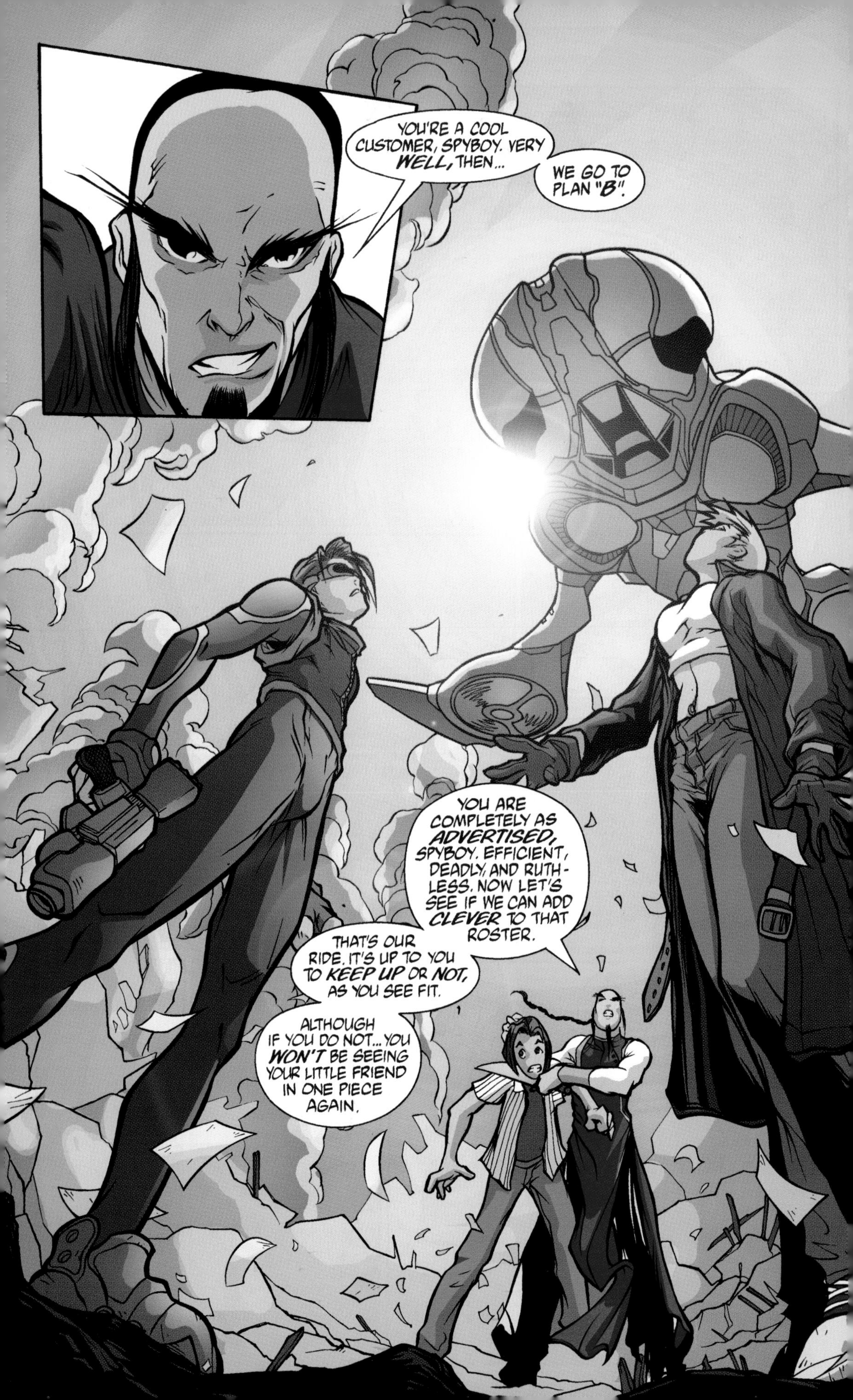
YOU'RE A COOL CUSTOMER, SPYBOY. VERY WELL, THEN...
WE GO TO PLAN "B".
YOU ARE COMPLETELY AS ADVERTISED, SPYBOY. EFFICIENT, DEADLY, AND RUTH-LESS. NOW LET'S SEE IF WE CAN ADD CLEVER TO THAT ROSTER.
THAT'S OUR RIDE. IT'S UP TO YOU TO KEEP UP OR NOT, AS YOU SEE FIT.
ALTHOUGH IF YOU DO NOT... YOU WON'T BE SEEING YOUR LITTLE FRIEND IN ONE PIECE AGAIN.

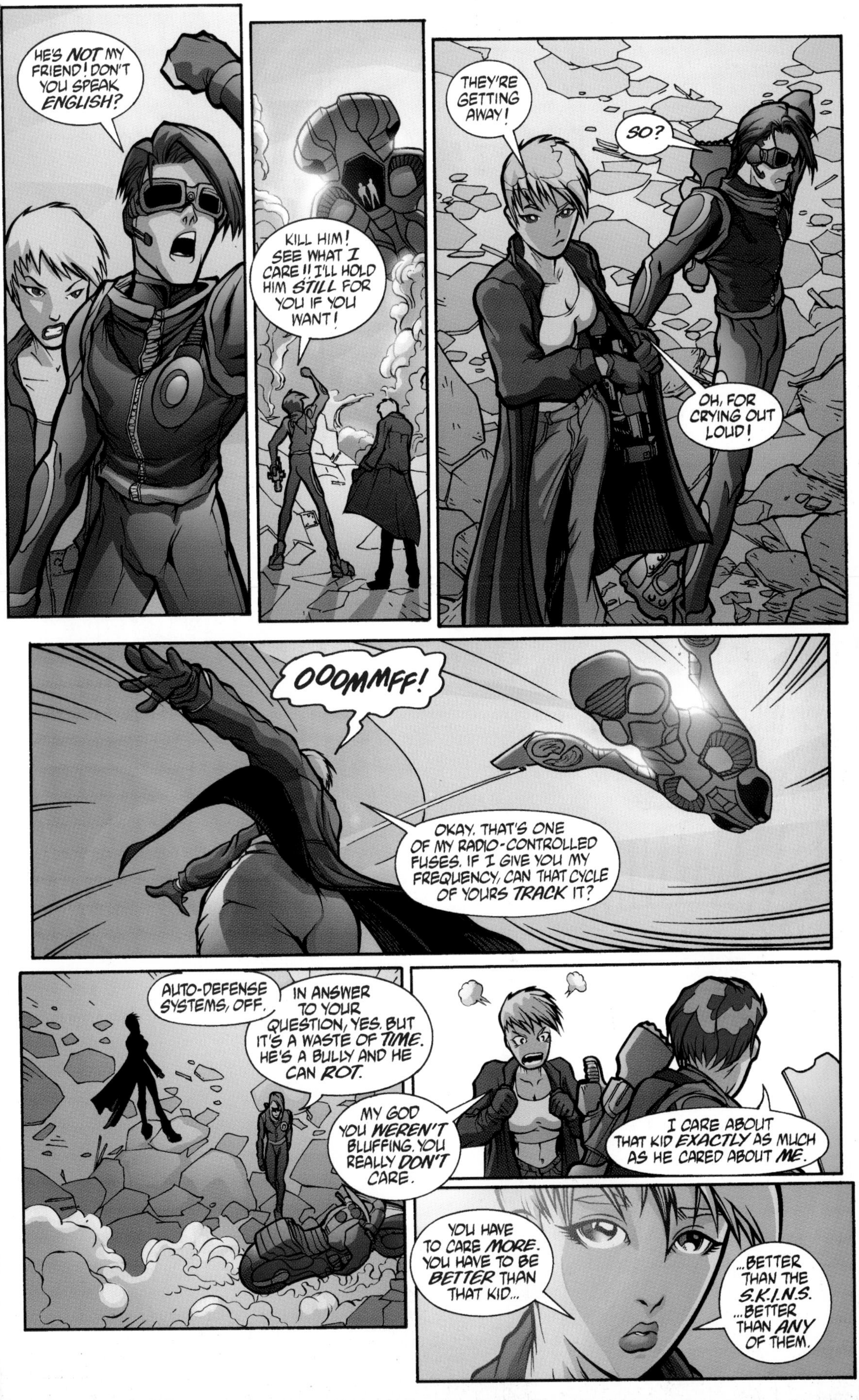
HE'S NOT MY FRIEND! DON'T YOU SPEAK ENGLISH?
KILL HIM! SEE WHAT I CARE!! I'LL HOLD HIM STILL FOR YOU IF YOU WANT!
THEY'RE GETTING AWAY!
SO?
OH, FOR CRYING OUT LOUD!
OOOMMFF!
OKAY. THAT'S ONE OF MY RADIO-CONTROLLED FUSES. IF I GIVE YOU MY FREQUENCY, CAN THAT CYCLE OF YOURS TRACK IT?
AUTO-DEFENSE SYSTEMS, OFF.
IN ANSWER TO YOUR QUESTION, YES. BUT IT'S A WASTE OF TIME. HE'S A BULLY AND HE CAN ROT.
MY GOD YOU WEREN'T BLUFFING. YOU REALLY DON'T CARE.
I CARE ABOUT THAT KID EXACTLY AS MUCH AS HE CARED ABOUT ME.
YOU HAVE TO CARE MORE. YOU HAVE TO BE BETTER THAN THAT KID...
...BETTER THAN THE S.K.I.N.S. ...BETTER THAN ANY OF THEM.

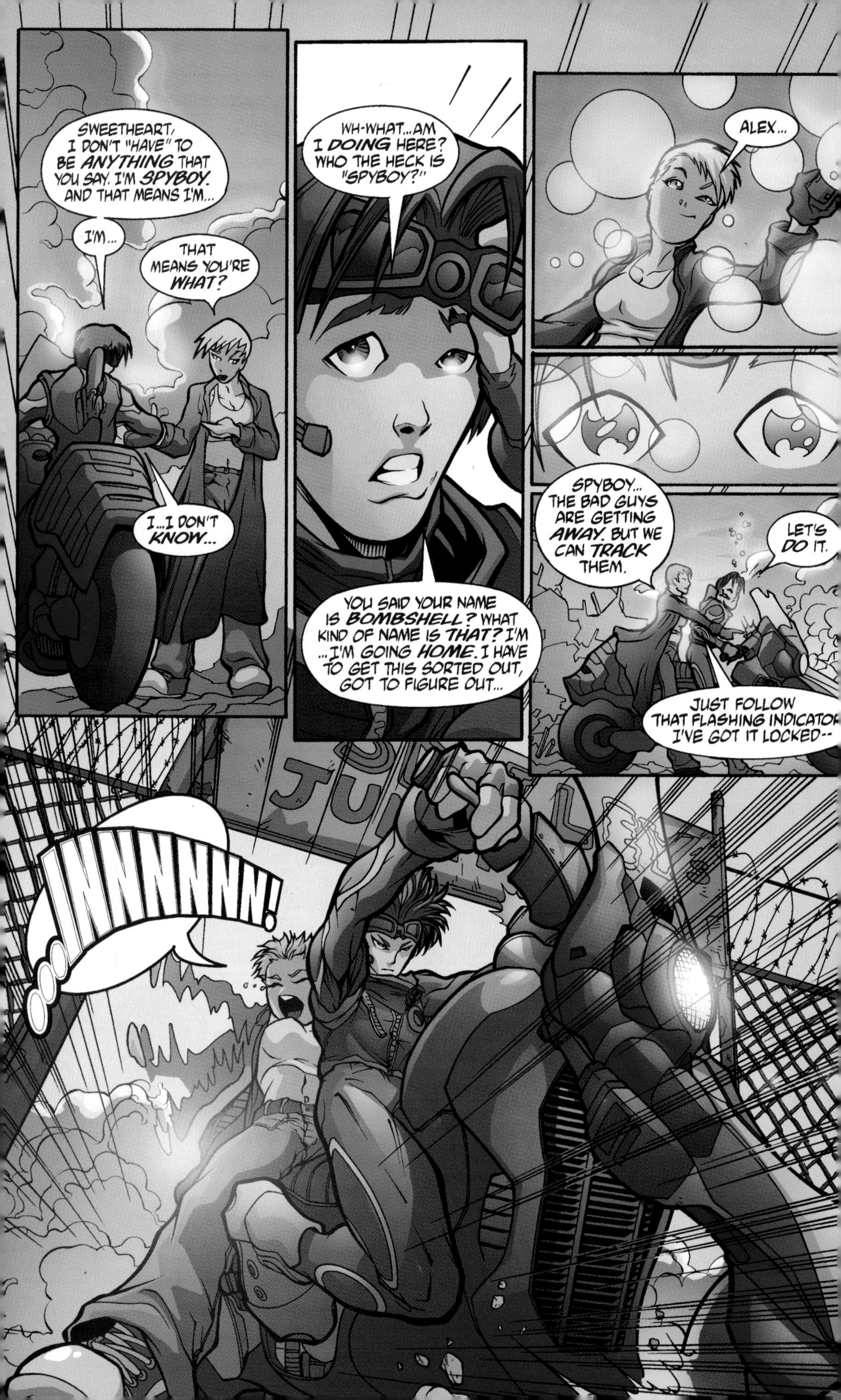

SWEETHEART, I DON'T "HAVE" TO BE ANYTHING THAT YOU SAY. I'M SPYBOY. AND THAT MEANS I'M...
I'M...
THAT MEANS YOU'RE WHAT?
I...I DON'T KNOW...
WH-WHAT...AM I DOING HERE? WHO THE HECK IS "SPYBOY?"
YOU SAID YOUR NAME IS BOMBSHELL? WHAT KIND OF NAME IS THAT? I'M ...I'M GOING HOME. I HAVE TO GET THIS SORTED OUT, GOT TO FIGURE OUT...
ALEX...
SPYBOY... THE BAD GUYS ARE GETTING AWAY. BUT WE CAN TRACK THEM.
LET'S DO IT.
JUST FOLLOW THAT FLASHING INDICATOR I'VE GOT IT LOCKED--
...INNNNNNN!

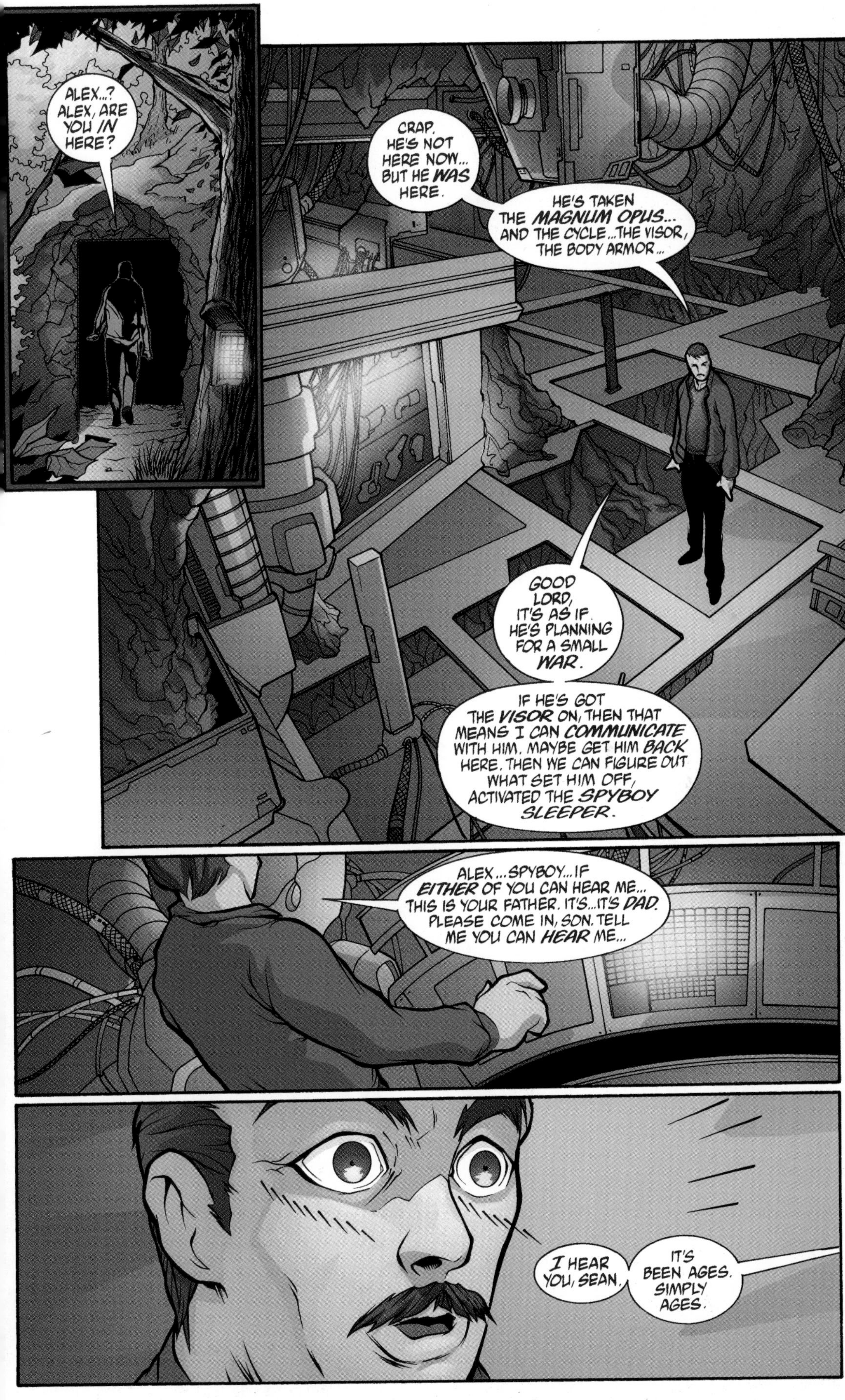
ALEX...? ALEX, ARE YOU IN HERE?
CRAP. HE'S NOT HERE NOW... BUT HE WAS HERE.
HE'S TAKEN THE MAGNUM OPUS... AND THE CYCLE...THE VISOR, THE BODY ARMOR...
GOOD LORD, IT'S AS IF HE'S PLANNING FOR A SMALL WAR.
IF HE'S GOT THE VISOR ON, THEN THAT MEANS I CAN COMMUNICATE WITH HIM. MAYBE GET HIM BACK HERE. THEN WE CAN FIGURE OUT WHAT SET HIM OFF, ACTIVATED THE SPYBOY SLEEPER.
ALEX...SPYBOY...IF EITHER OF YOU CAN HEAR ME... THIS IS YOUR FATHER. IT'S...IT'S DAD. PLEASE COME IN, SON. TELL ME YOU CAN HEAR ME...
I HEAR YOU, SEAN.
IT'S BEEN AGES. SIMPLY AGES.

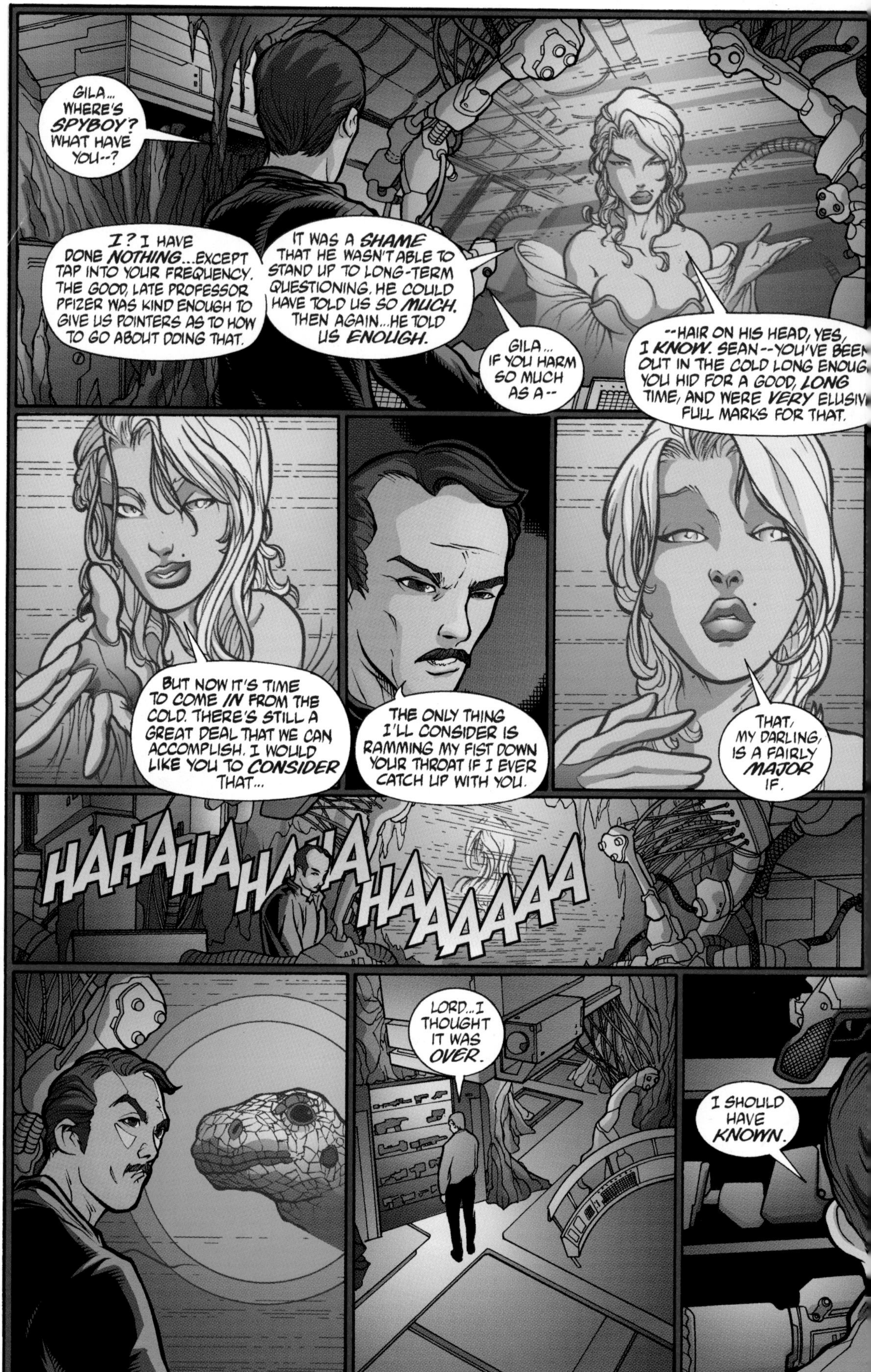

GILA... WHERE'S SPYBOY? WHAT HAVE YOU--?
I? I HAVE DONE NOTHING...EXCEPT TAP INTO YOUR FREQUENCY. THE GOOD, LATE PROFESSOR PFIZER WAS KIND ENOUGH TO GIVE US POINTERS AS TO HOW TO GO ABOUT DOING THAT.
IT WAS A SHAME THAT HE WASN'T ABLE TO STAND UP TO LONG-TERM QUESTIONING. HE COULD HAVE TOLD US SO MUCH. THEN AGAIN...HE TOLD US ENOUGH.
GILA... IF YOU HARM SO MUCH AS A--
--HAIR ON HIS HEAD, YES, I KNOW. SEAN--YOU'VE BEEN OUT IN THE COLD LONG ENOUGH. YOU HID FOR A GOOD, LONG TIME, AND WERE VERY ELUSIVE. FULL MARKS FOR THAT.
BUT NOW IT'S TIME TO COME IN FROM THE COLD. THERE'S STILL A GREAT DEAL THAT WE CAN ACCOMPLISH. I WOULD LIKE YOU TO CONSIDER THAT...
THE ONLY THING I'LL CONSIDER IS RAMMING MY FIST DOWN YOUR THROAT IF I EVER CATCH UP WITH YOU.
THAT, MY DARLING, IS A FAIRLY MAJOR IF.
HAHAHAHAHAHAHAAAAAA
LORD...I THOUGHT IT WAS OVER.
I SHOULD HAVE KNOWN.

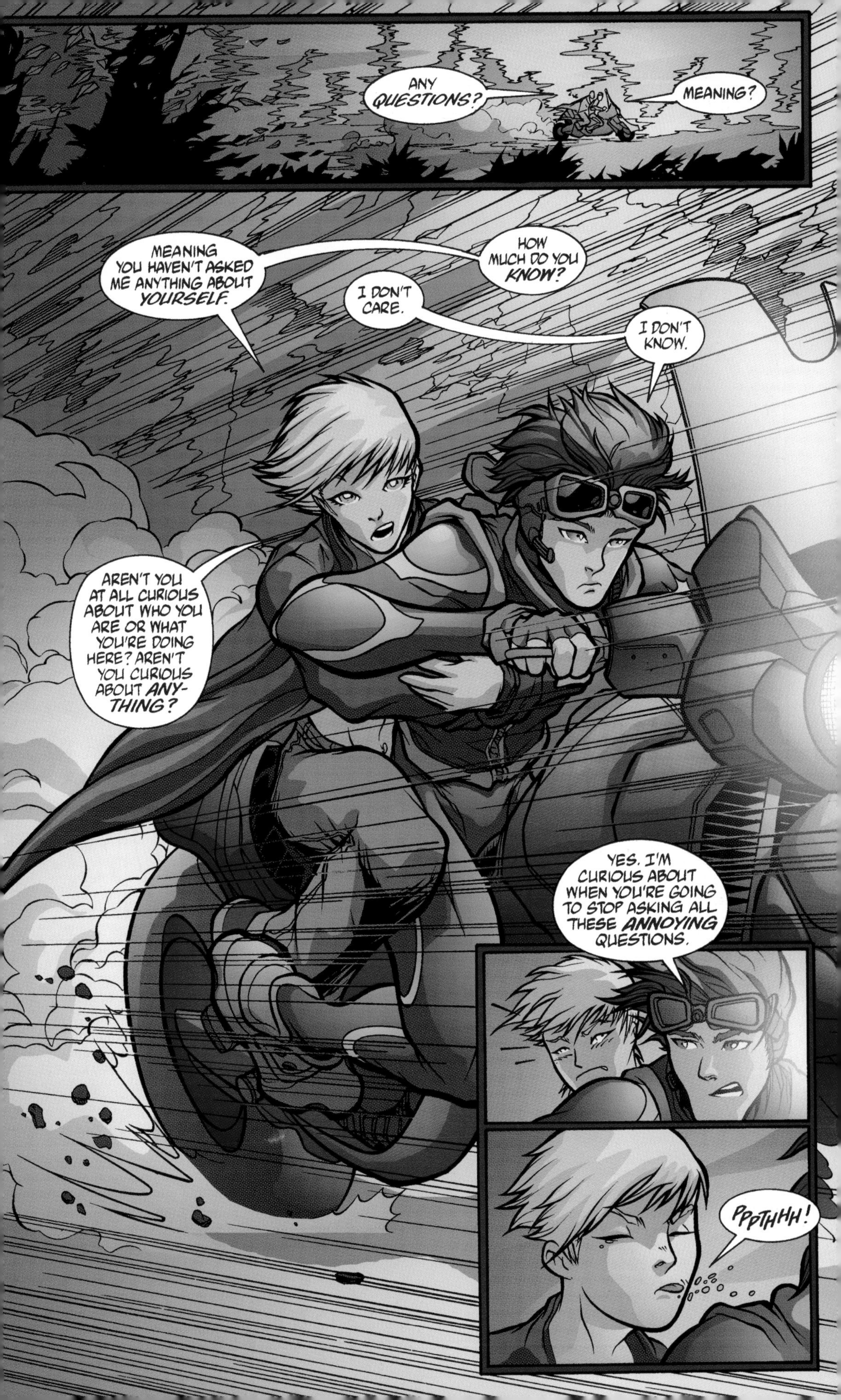
ANY QUESTIONS?
MEANING?
MEANING YOU HAVEN'T ASKED ME ANYTHING ABOUT YOURSELF.
HOW MUCH DO YOU KNOW?
I DON'T CARE.
I DON'T KNOW.
AREN'T YOU AT ALL CURIOUS ABOUT WHO YOU ARE OR WHAT YOU'RE DOING HERE? AREN'T YOU CURIOUS ABOUT ANY-THING?
YES. I'M CURIOUS ABOUT WHEN YOU'RE GOING TO STOP ASKING ALL THESE ANNOYING QUESTIONS.
PPPTHHH!

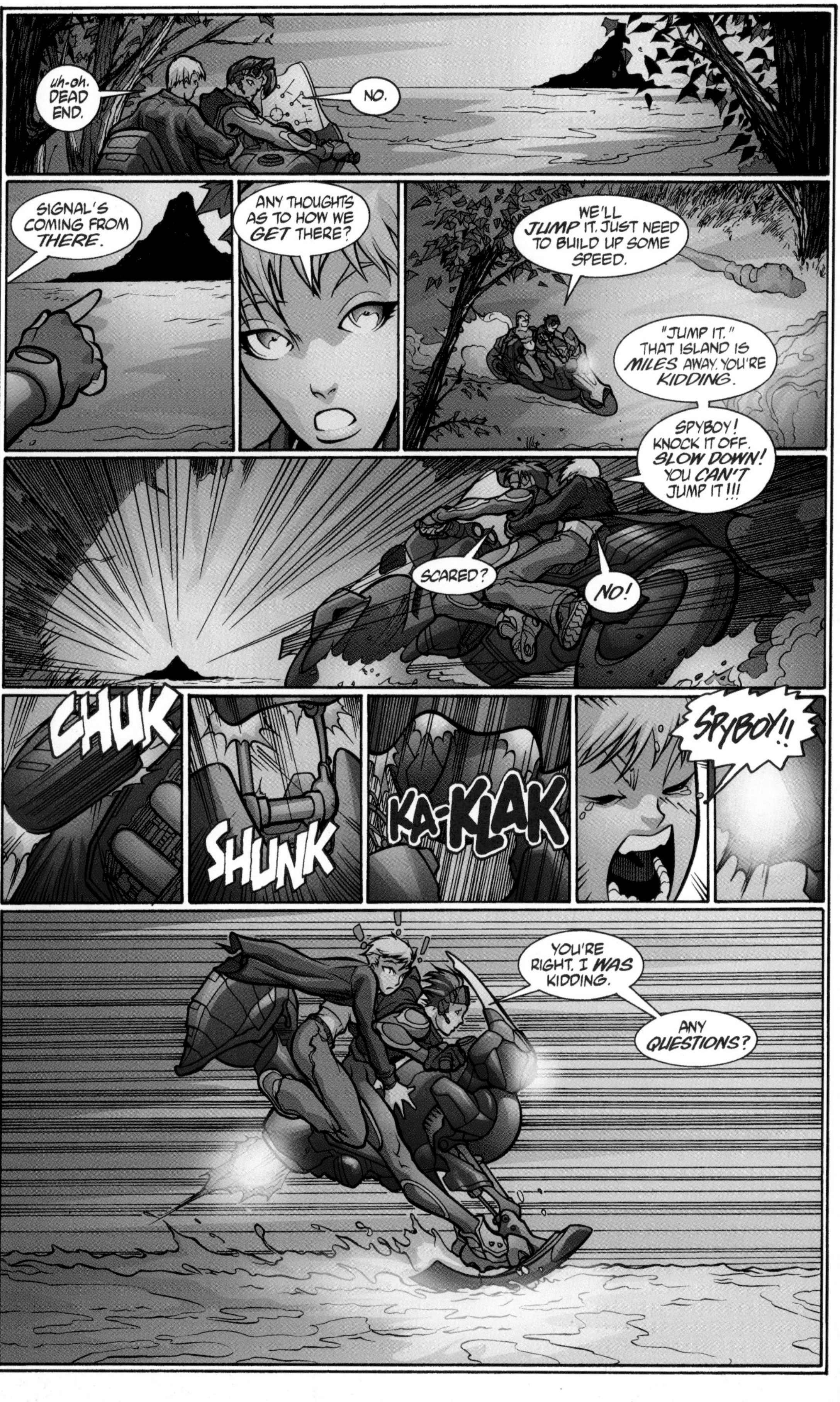
uh-oh. DEAD END.
NO.
SIGNAL'S COMING FROM THERE.
ANY THOUGHTS AS TO HOW WE GET THERE?
WE'LL JUMP IT. JUST NEED TO BUILD UP SOME SPEED.
"JUMP IT." THAT ISLAND IS MILES AWAY. YOU'RE KIDDING.
SPYBOY! KNOCK IT OFF. SLOW DOWN! YOU CAN'T JUMP IT!!!
SCARED?
NO!
CHUK
SHUNK
KA-KLAK
SPYBOY!!
YOU'RE RIGHT. I WAS KIDDING.
ANY QUESTIONS?

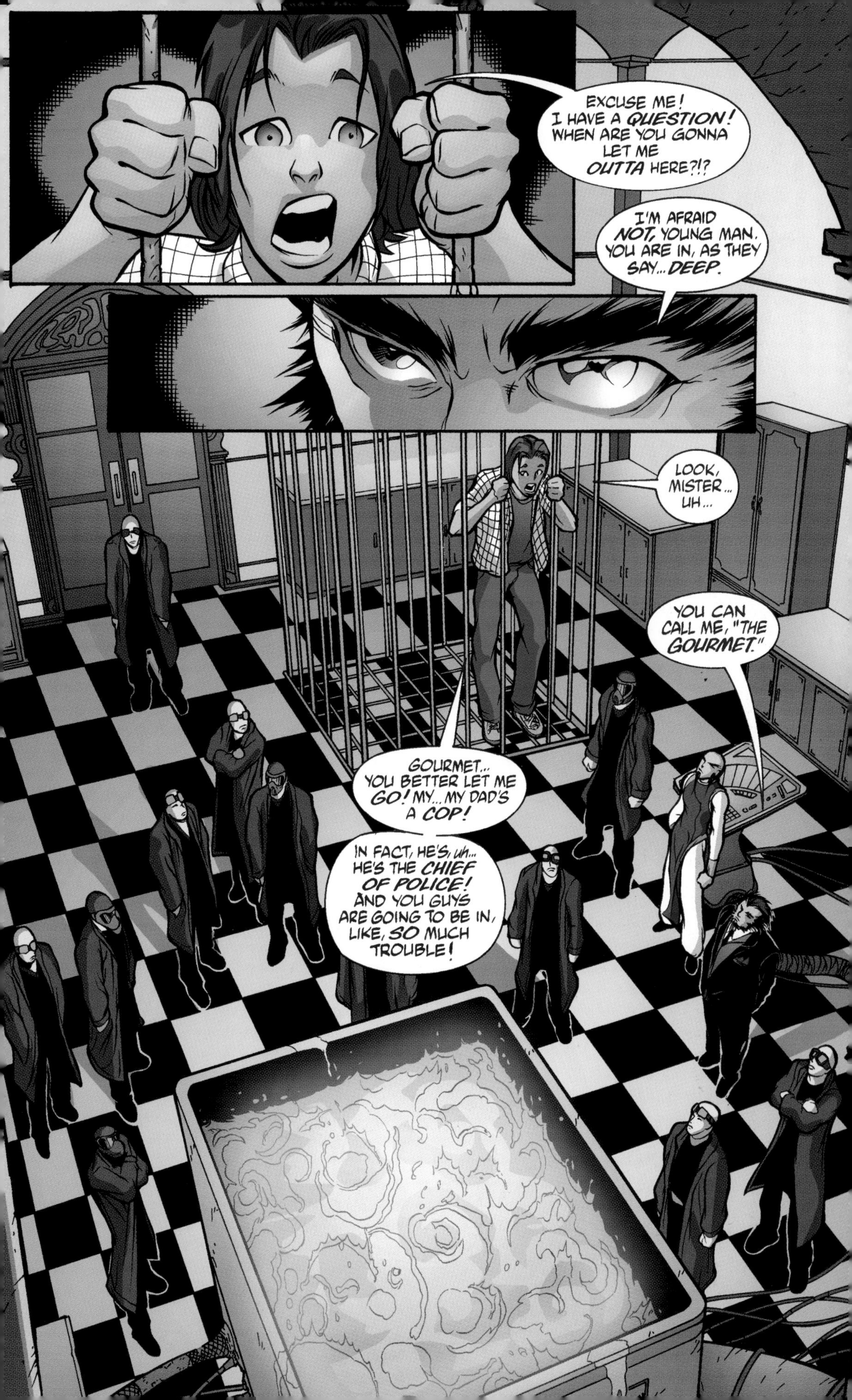
EXCUSE ME! I HAVE A QUESTION! WHEN ARE YOU GONNA LET ME OUTTA HERE?!?
I'M AFRAID NOT, YOUNG MAN. YOU ARE IN, AS THEY SAY... DEEP.
LOOK, MISTER... UH...
YOU CAN CALL ME, "THE GOURMET."
GOURMET... YOU BETTER LET ME GO! MY... MY DAD'S A COP!
IN FACT, HE'S, uh... HE'S THE CHIEF OF POLICE! AND YOU GUYS ARE GOING TO BE IN, LIKE, SO MUCH TROUBLE!

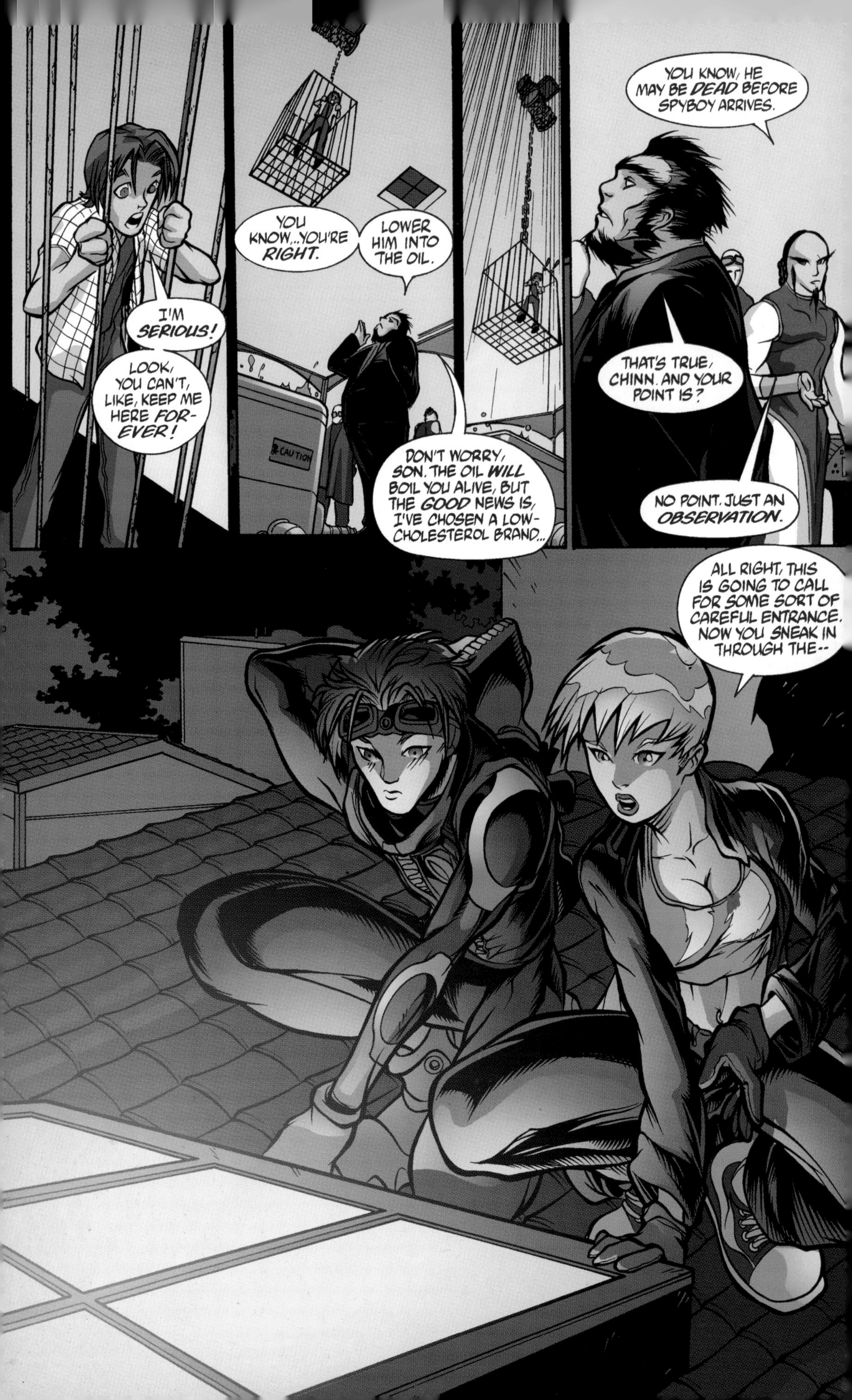
I'M SERIOUS!
LOOK, YOU CAN'T, LIKE, KEEP ME HERE FOR-EVER!
YOU KNOW...YOU'RE RIGHT.
LOWER HIM INTO THE OIL.
CAUTION
DON'T WORRY, SON. THE OIL WILL BOIL YOU ALIVE, BUT THE GOOD NEWS IS, I'VE CHOSEN A LOW-CHOLESTEROL BRAND...
YOU KNOW, HE MAY BE DEAD BEFORE SPYBOY ARRIVES.
THAT'S TRUE, CHINN. AND YOUR POINT IS?
NO POINT. JUST AN OBSERVATION.
ALL RIGHT, THIS IS GOING TO CALL FOR SOME SORT OF CAREFUL ENTRANCE. NOW YOU SNEAK IN THROUGH THE--

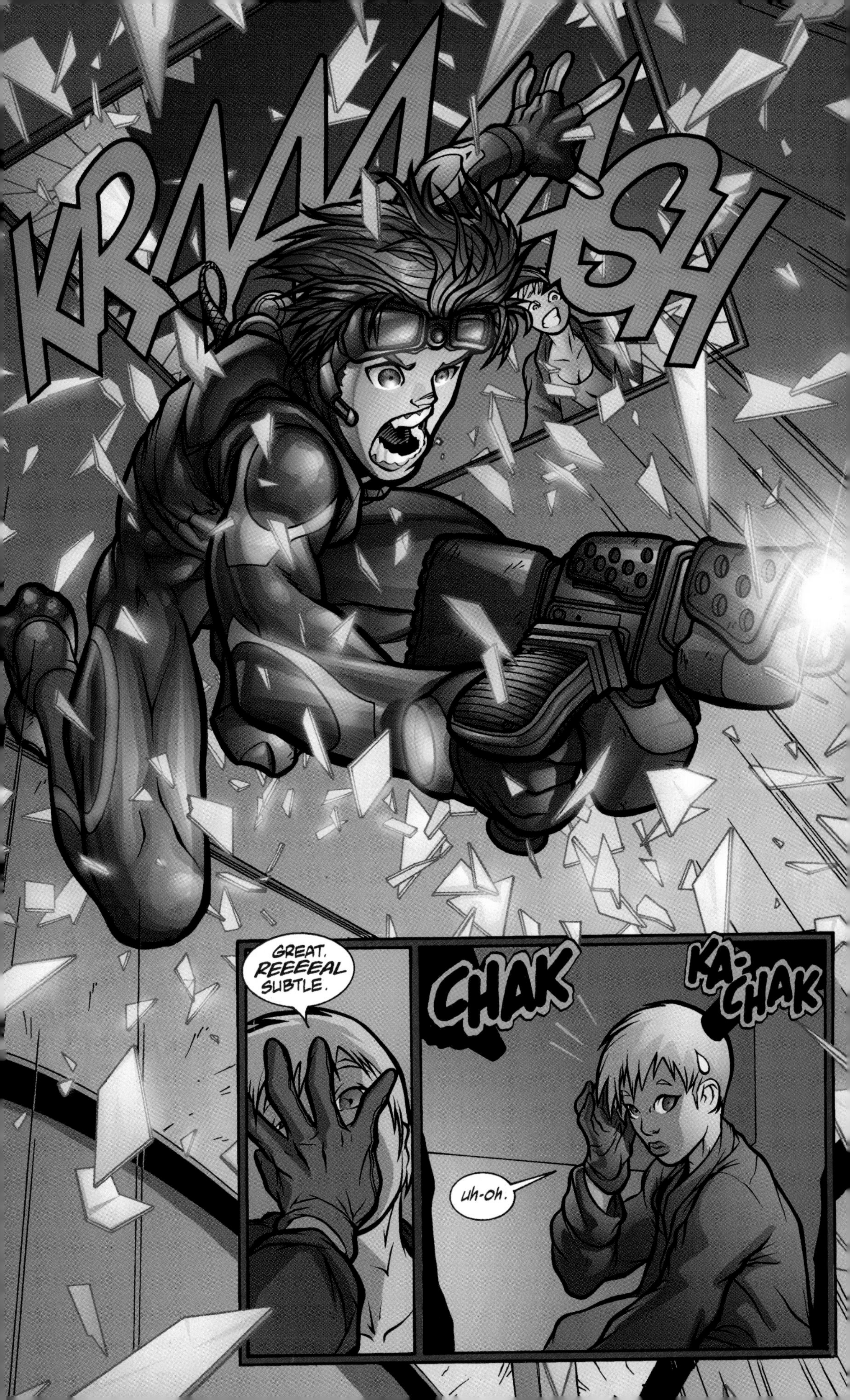
KRAAAAASH
GREAT. REEEEAL SUBTLE.
CHAK
KA-CHAK
uh-oh.

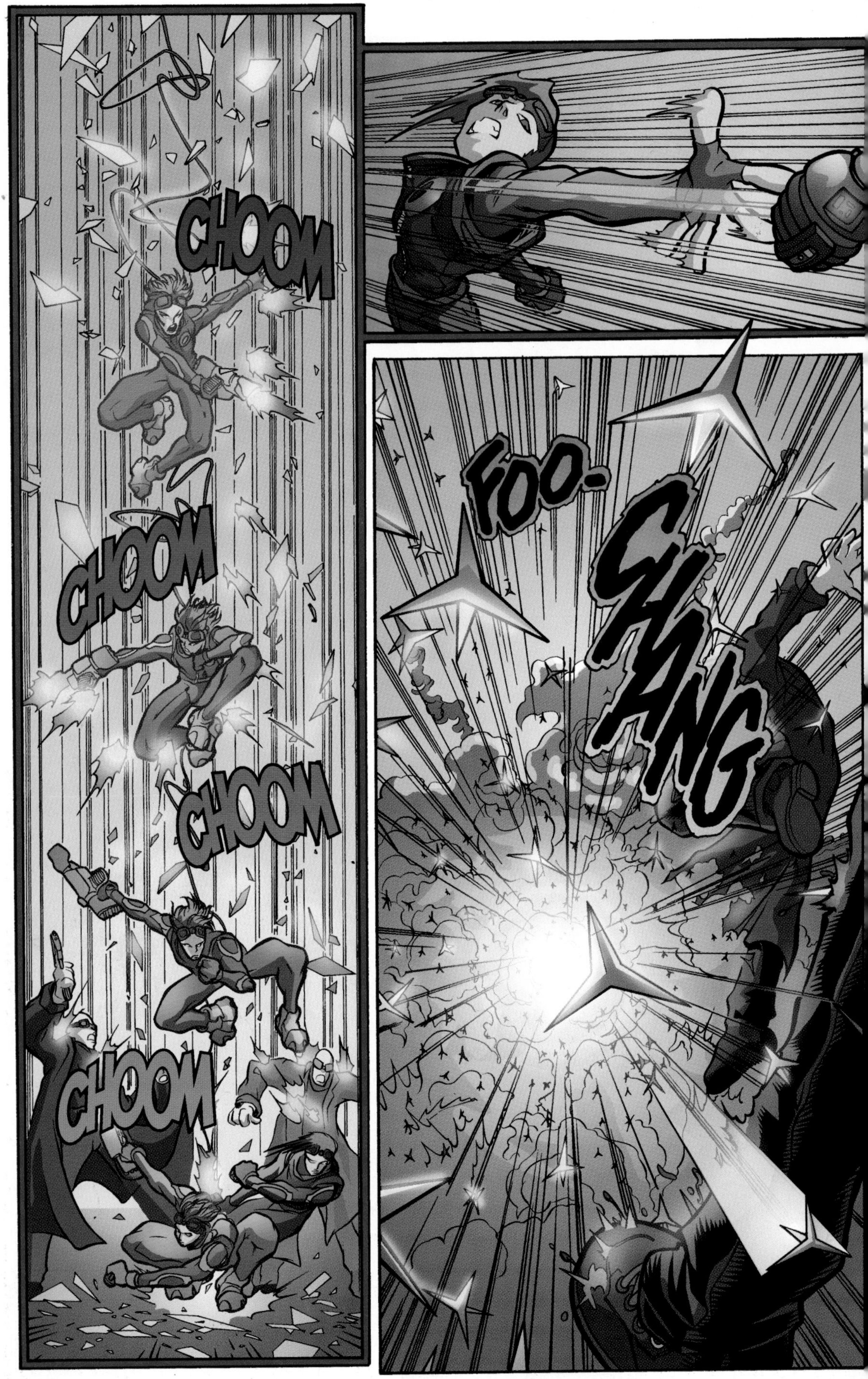
CHOOM
CHOOM
CHOOM
CHOOM
FOO-
CHANG

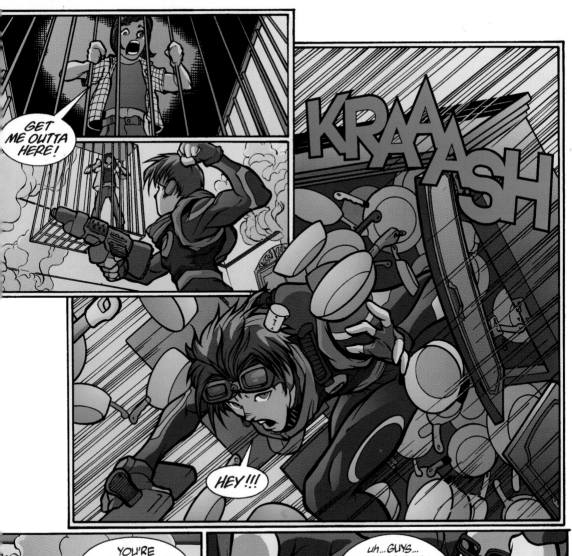

GET ME OUTTA HERE!

KRAAASH

HEY!!!

YOU'RE QUITE *SKILLED*, SPYBOY. BUT I HAD THE *SUPERIOR SKILLET.*

HAUL HIM *OUT* FROM THERE.

uh... GUYS... LOOK... I THINK WE HAVE A BIT OF A *MISUNDERSTAND-ING* HERE.

PERHAPS *NOT.* CHINN, STOP HIS FRIEND'S *DESCENT,* PLEASE.

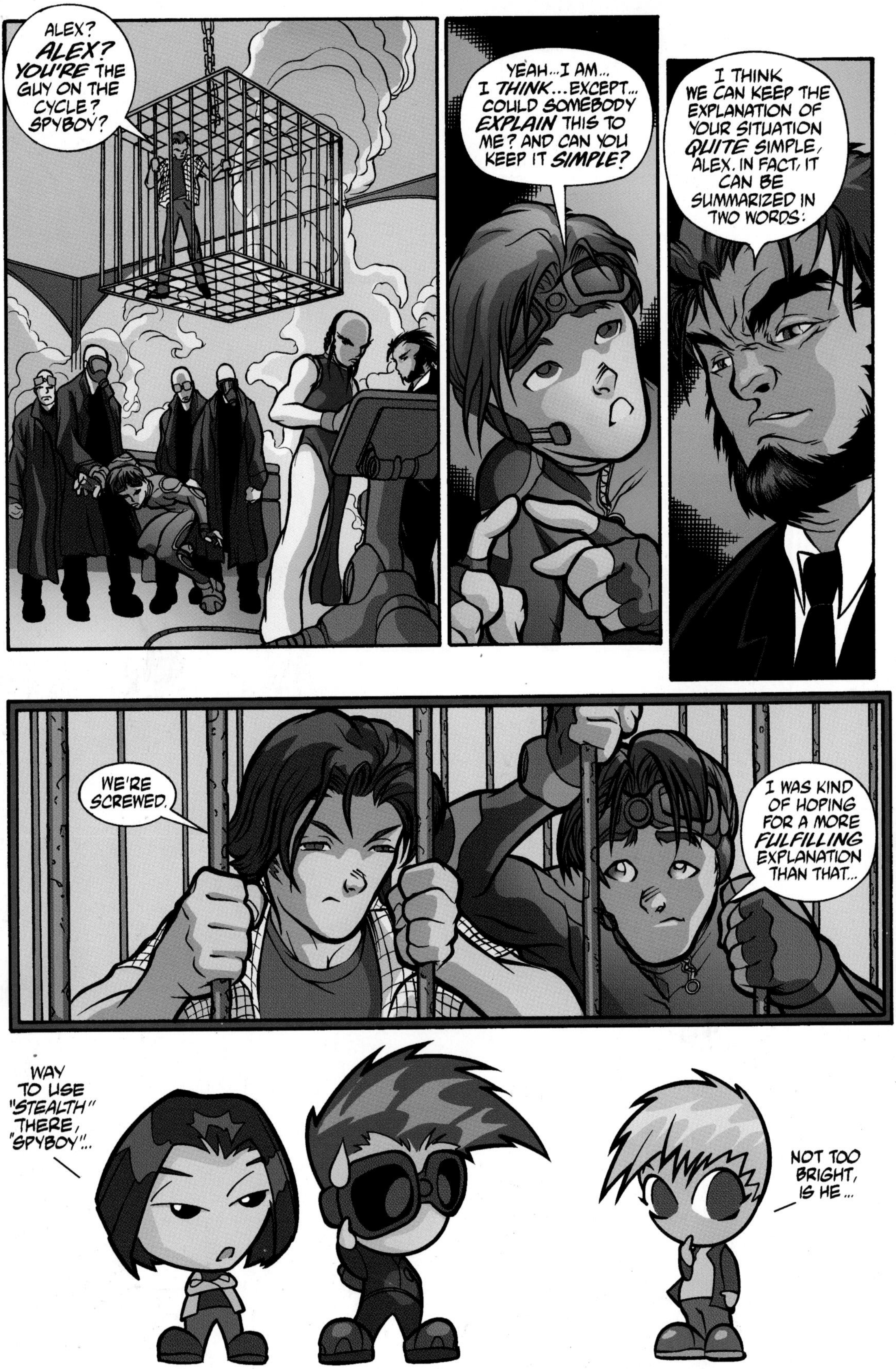
ALEX? ALEX? YOU'RE THE GUY ON THE CYCLE? SPYBOY?
YEAH...I AM... I THINK...EXCEPT... COULD SOMEBODY EXPLAIN THIS TO ME? AND CAN YOU KEEP IT SIMPLE?
I THINK WE CAN KEEP THE EXPLANATION OF YOUR SITUATION QUITE SIMPLE, ALEX. IN FACT, IT CAN BE SUMMARIZED IN TWO WORDS:
WE'RE SCREWED.
I WAS KIND OF HOPING FOR A MORE FULFILLING EXPLANATION THAN THAT...
WAY TO USE "STEALTH" THERE, "SPYBOY"...
NOT TOO BRIGHT, IS HE...

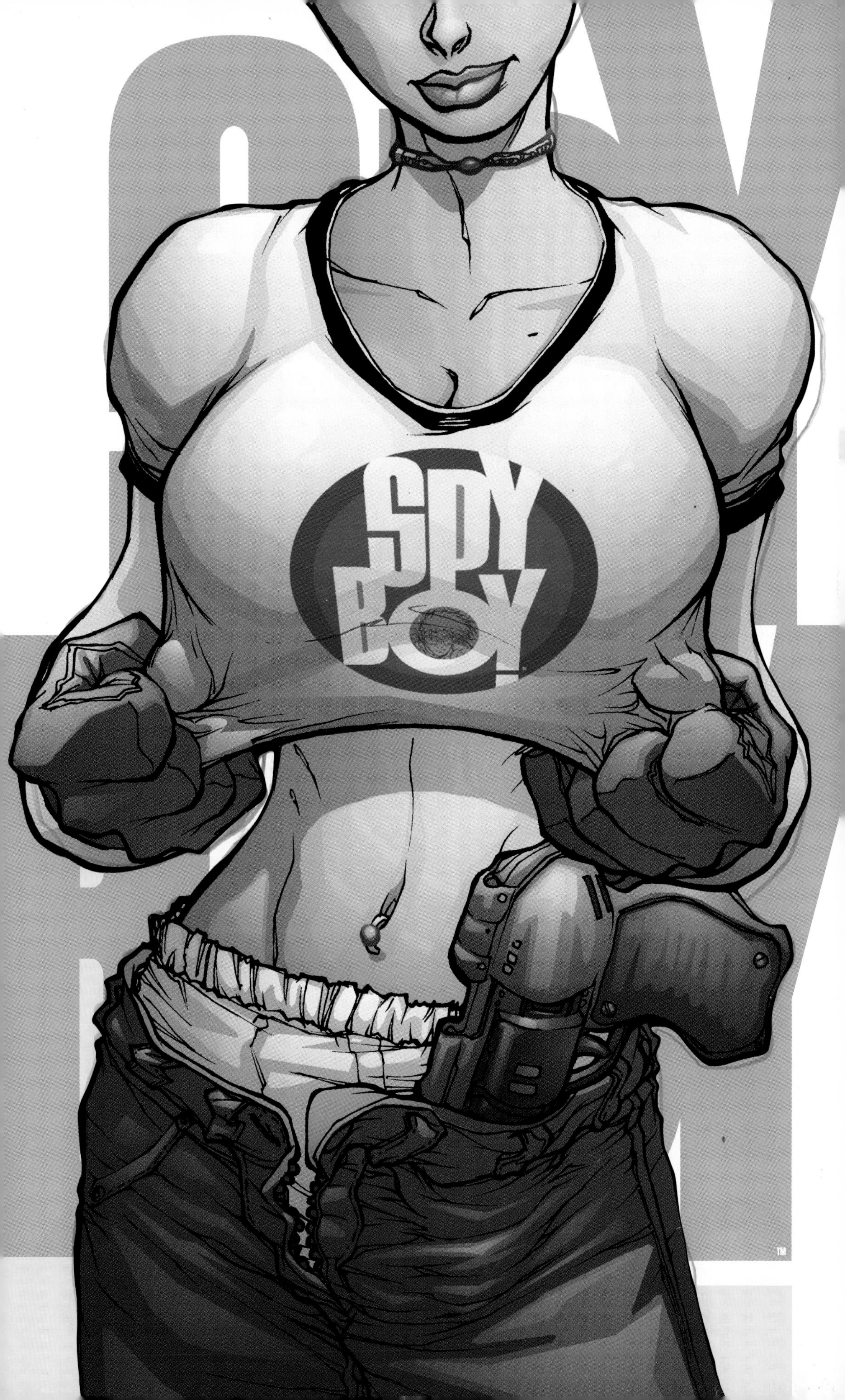
SPY BOY

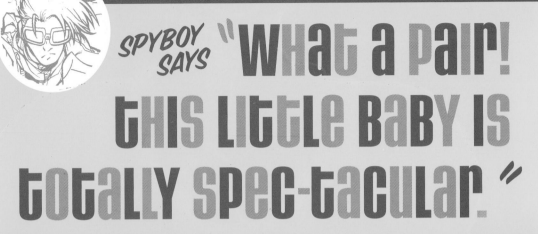

SPYBOY SAYS "WHAT A PAIR! THIS LITTLE BABY IS TOTALLY SPEC-TACULAR."

- NO, he's not talking about **BOMBSHELL**, he means . . .

NO SPY SHOULD BE SEEN WITHOUT IT!

- THERMAL, INFRARED AND ULTRAVIOLET NIGHT VISION
- TRANSMITTER/RECEIVER
- AUTOMATIC WEAPON TARGETING

SPYBOY'S SPY ★ GOGGLES

CREATED FOR **S.H.I.R.T.S.** BY Hach & Busch CYBER-OPTIC INDUSTRIES "Face Furniture from the future!"

3 "FROM RUSSIA, WITH FRIES AND A COKE"

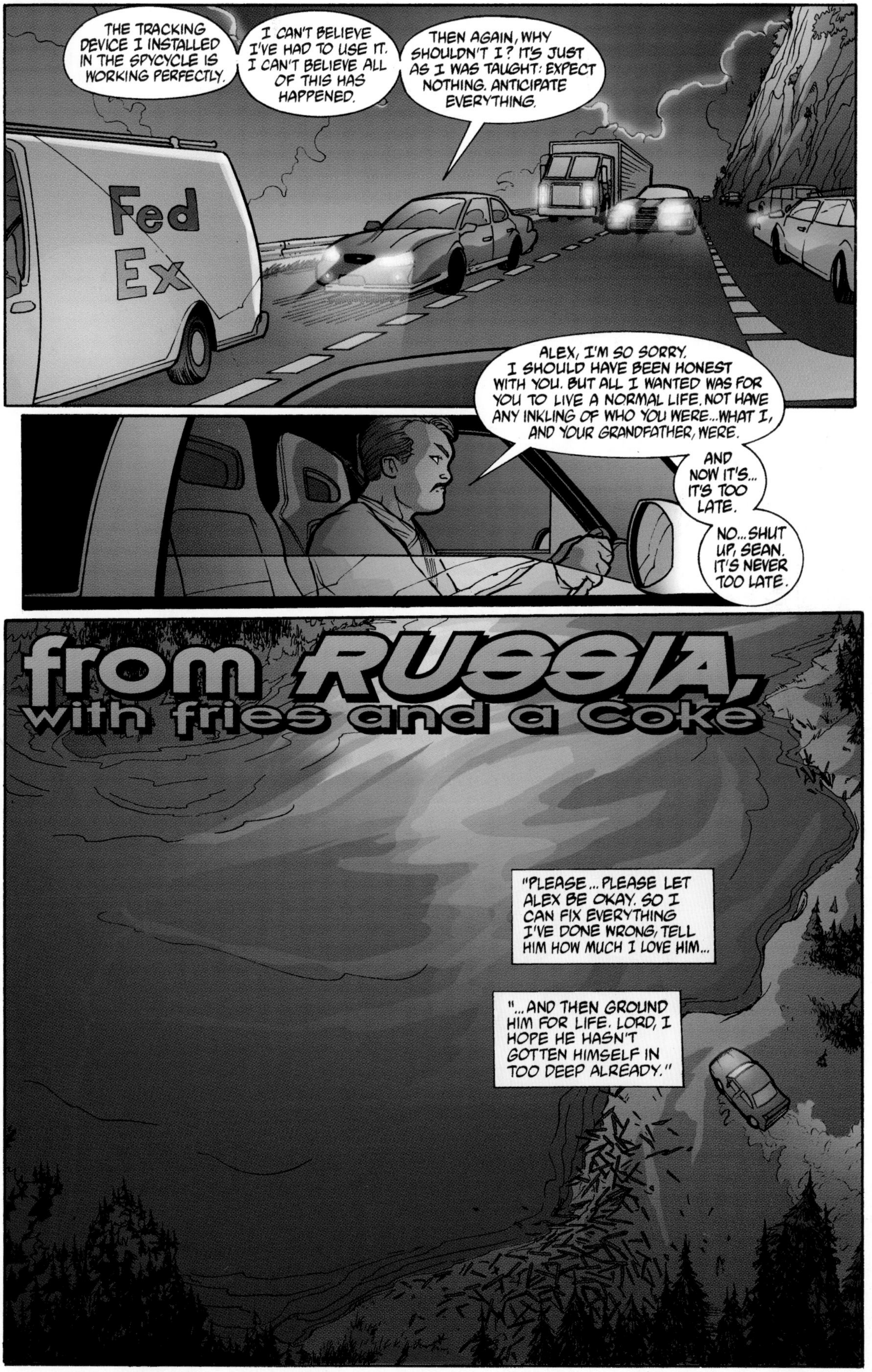
THE TRACKING DEVICE I INSTALLED IN THE SPYCYCLE IS WORKING PERFECTLY.
I CAN'T BELIEVE I'VE HAD TO USE IT. I CAN'T BELIEVE ALL OF THIS HAS HAPPENED.
THEN AGAIN, WHY SHOULDN'T I? IT'S JUST AS I WAS TAUGHT: EXPECT NOTHING. ANTICIPATE EVERYTHING.
Fed Ex
ALEX, I'M SO SORRY. I SHOULD HAVE BEEN HONEST WITH YOU. BUT ALL I WANTED WAS FOR YOU TO LIVE A NORMAL LIFE. NOT HAVE ANY INKLING OF WHO YOU WERE...WHAT I, AND YOUR GRANDFATHER, WERE.
AND NOW IT'S... IT'S TOO LATE.
NO...SHUT UP, SEAN. IT'S NEVER TOO LATE.
from RUSSIA, with fries and a Coke
"PLEASE... PLEASE LET ALEX BE OKAY. SO I CAN FIX EVERYTHING I'VE DONE WRONG, TELL HIM HOW MUCH I LOVE HIM...
"...AND THEN GROUND HIM FOR LIFE. LORD, I HOPE HE HASN'T GOTTEN HIMSELF IN TOO DEEP ALREADY."

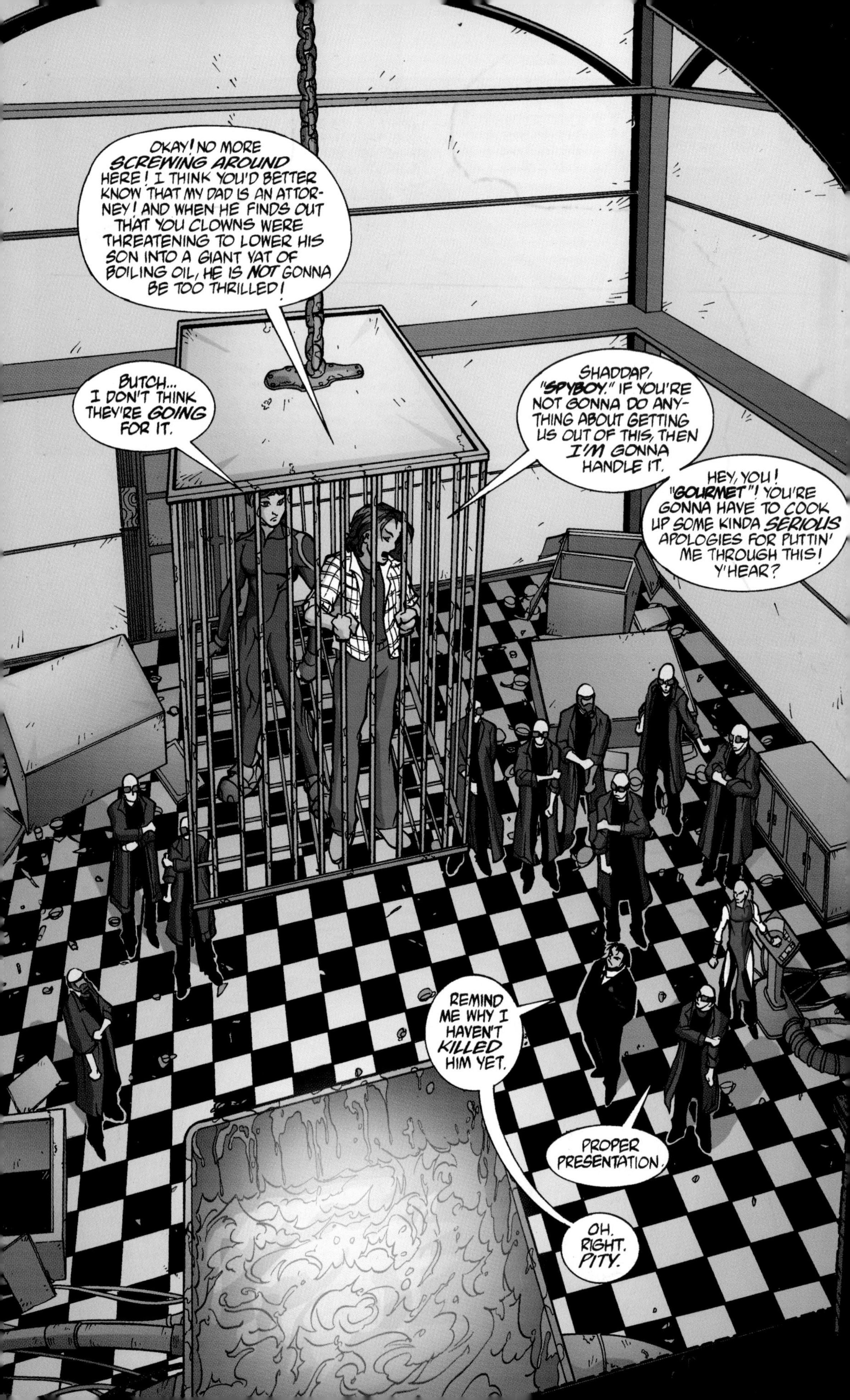
OKAY! NO MORE SCREWING AROUND HERE! I THINK YOU'D BETTER KNOW THAT MY DAD IS AN ATTORNEY! AND WHEN HE FINDS OUT THAT YOU CLOWNS WERE THREATENING TO LOWER HIS SON INTO A GIANT VAT OF BOILING OIL, HE IS NOT GONNA BE TOO THRILLED!
BUTCH... I DON'T THINK THEY'RE GOING FOR IT.
SHADDAP, "SPYBOY." IF YOU'RE NOT GONNA DO ANYTHING ABOUT GETTING US OUT OF THIS, THEN I'M GONNA HANDLE IT.
HEY, YOU! "GOURMET"! YOU'RE GONNA HAVE TO COOK UP SOME KINDA SERIOUS APOLOGIES FOR PUTTIN' ME THROUGH THIS! Y'HEAR?
REMIND ME WHY I HAVEN'T KILLED HIM YET.
PROPER PRESENTATION.
OH. RIGHT. PITY.

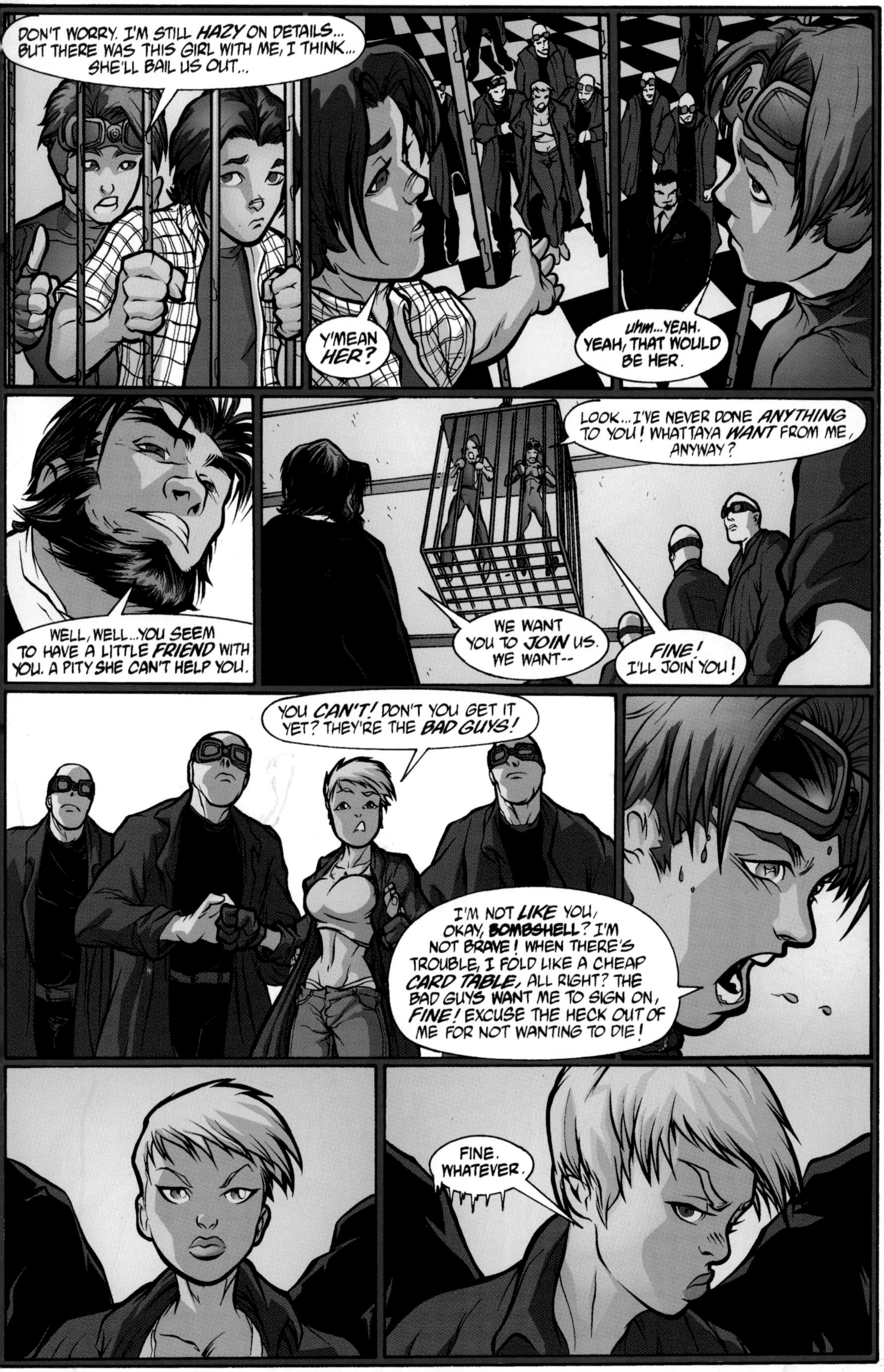
DON'T WORRY. I'M STILL HAZY ON DETAILS... BUT THERE WAS THIS GIRL WITH ME, I THINK... SHE'LL BAIL US OUT...
Y'MEAN HER?
uhm...YEAH. YEAH, THAT WOULD BE HER.
WELL, WELL...YOU SEEM TO HAVE A LITTLE FRIEND WITH YOU. A PITY SHE CAN'T HELP YOU.
LOOK...I'VE NEVER DONE ANYTHING TO YOU! WHATTAYA WANT FROM ME, ANYWAY?
WE WANT YOU TO JOIN US. WE WANT--
FINE! I'LL JOIN YOU!
YOU CAN'T! DON'T YOU GET IT YET? THEY'RE THE BAD GUYS!
I'M NOT LIKE YOU, OKAY, BOMBSHELL? I'M NOT BRAVE! WHEN THERE'S TROUBLE, I FOLD LIKE A CHEAP CARD TABLE, ALL RIGHT? THE BAD GUYS WANT ME TO SIGN ON, FINE! EXCUSE THE HECK OUT OF ME FOR NOT WANTING TO DIE!
FINE. WHATEVER.

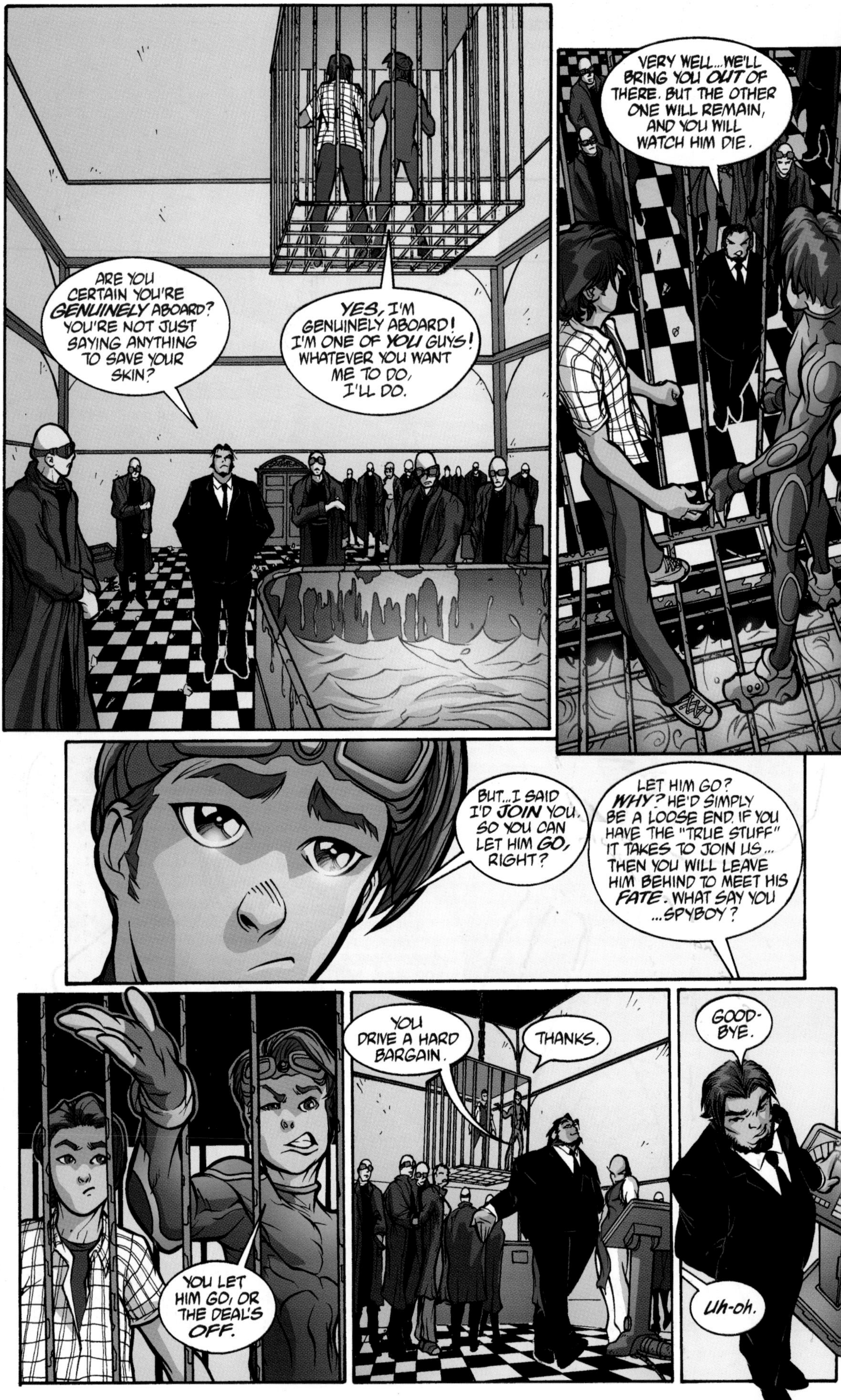
ARE YOU CERTAIN YOU'RE GENUINELY ABOARD? YOU'RE NOT JUST SAYING ANYTHING TO SAVE YOUR SKIN?
YES, I'M GENUINELY ABOARD! I'M ONE OF YOU GUYS! WHATEVER YOU WANT ME TO DO, I'LL DO.
VERY WELL...WE'LL BRING YOU OUT OF THERE. BUT THE OTHER ONE WILL REMAIN, AND YOU WILL WATCH HIM DIE.
BUT...I SAID I'D JOIN YOU. SO YOU CAN LET HIM GO, RIGHT?
LET HIM GO? WHY? HE'D SIMPLY BE A LOOSE END. IF YOU HAVE THE "TRUE STUFF" IT TAKES TO JOIN US... THEN YOU WILL LEAVE HIM BEHIND TO MEET HIS FATE. WHAT SAY YOU ...SPYBOY?
YOU LET HIM GO, OR THE DEAL'S OFF.
YOU DRIVE A HARD BARGAIN.
THANKS.
GOOD-BYE.
Uh-oh.

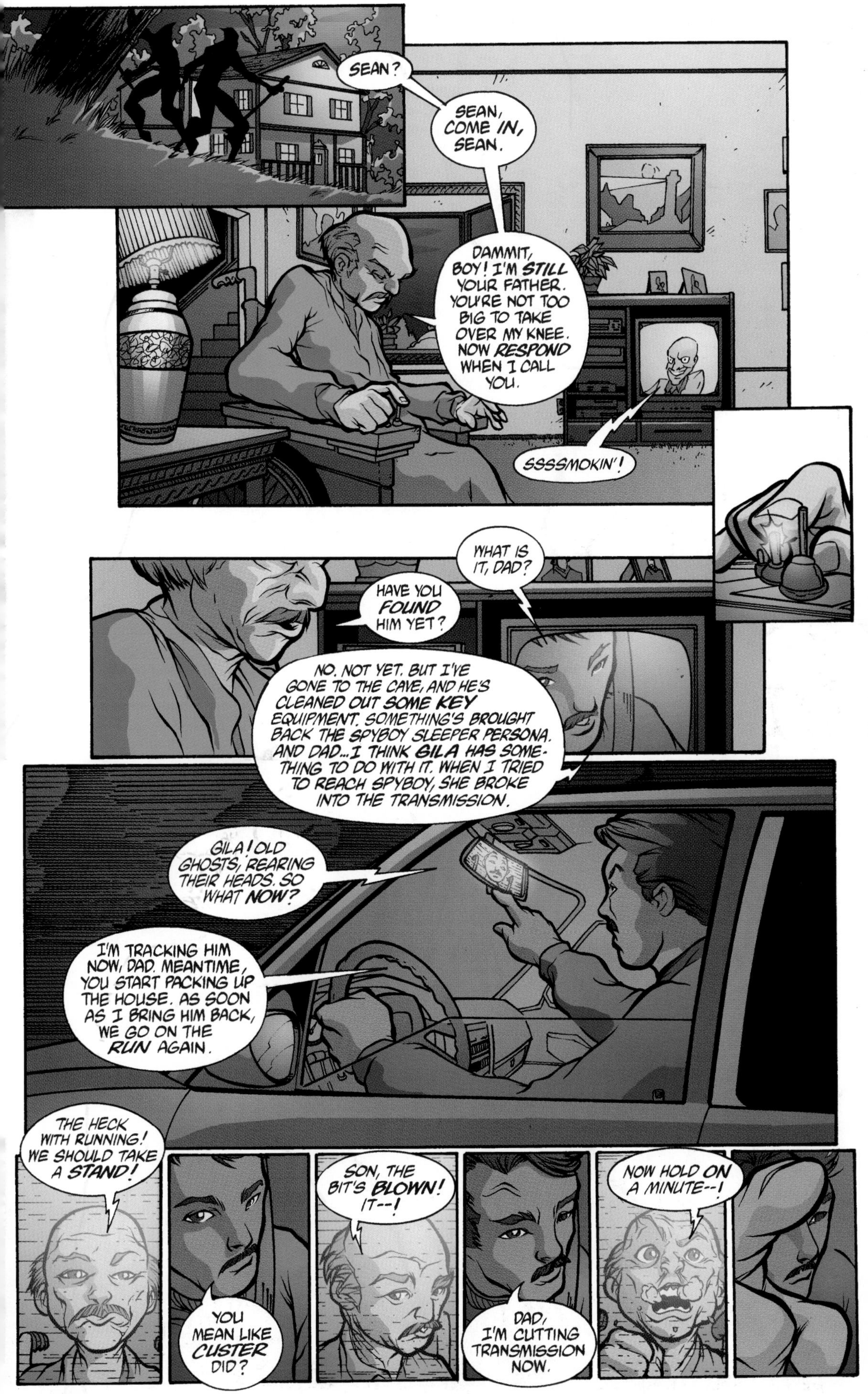
SEAN?
SEAN, COME IN, SEAN.
DAMMIT, BOY! I'M STILL YOUR FATHER. YOU'RE NOT TOO BIG TO TAKE OVER MY KNEE. NOW RESPOND WHEN I CALL YOU.
SSSSMOKIN'!
WHAT IS IT, DAD?
HAVE YOU FOUND HIM YET?
NO. NOT YET. BUT I'VE GONE TO THE CAVE, AND HE'S CLEANED OUT SOME KEY EQUIPMENT. SOMETHING'S BROUGHT BACK THE SPYBOY SLEEPER PERSONA. AND DAD...I THINK GILA HAS SOMETHING TO DO WITH IT. WHEN I TRIED TO REACH SPYBOY, SHE BROKE INTO THE TRANSMISSION.
GILA! OLD GHOSTS, REARING THEIR HEADS. SO WHAT NOW?
I'M TRACKING HIM NOW, DAD. MEANTIME, YOU START PACKING UP THE HOUSE. AS SOON AS I BRING HIM BACK, WE GO ON THE RUN AGAIN.
THE HECK WITH RUNNING! WE SHOULD TAKE A STAND!
YOU MEAN LIKE CUSTER DID?
SON, THE BIT'S BLOWN! IT--!
DAD, I'M CUTTING TRANSMISSION NOW.
NOW HOLD ON A MINUTE--!

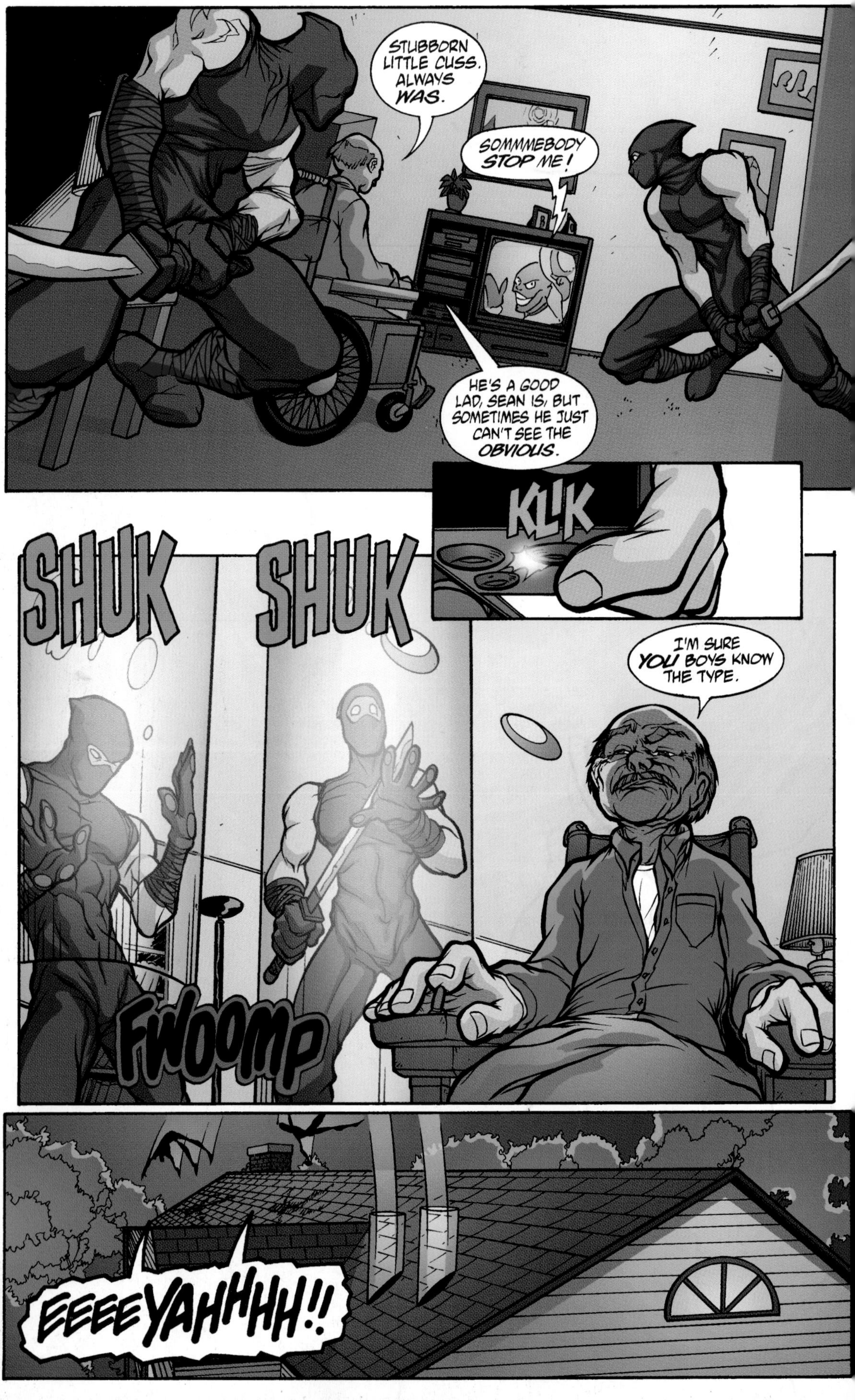

STUBBORN LITTLE CUSS. ALWAYS WAS.
SOMMMEBODY STOP ME!
HE'S A GOOD LAD, SEAN IS, BUT SOMETIMES HE JUST CAN'T SEE THE OBVIOUS.
KLIK
SHUK
SHUK
I'M SURE YOU BOYS KNOW THE TYPE.
FWOOMP
EEEEYAHHHHH!!

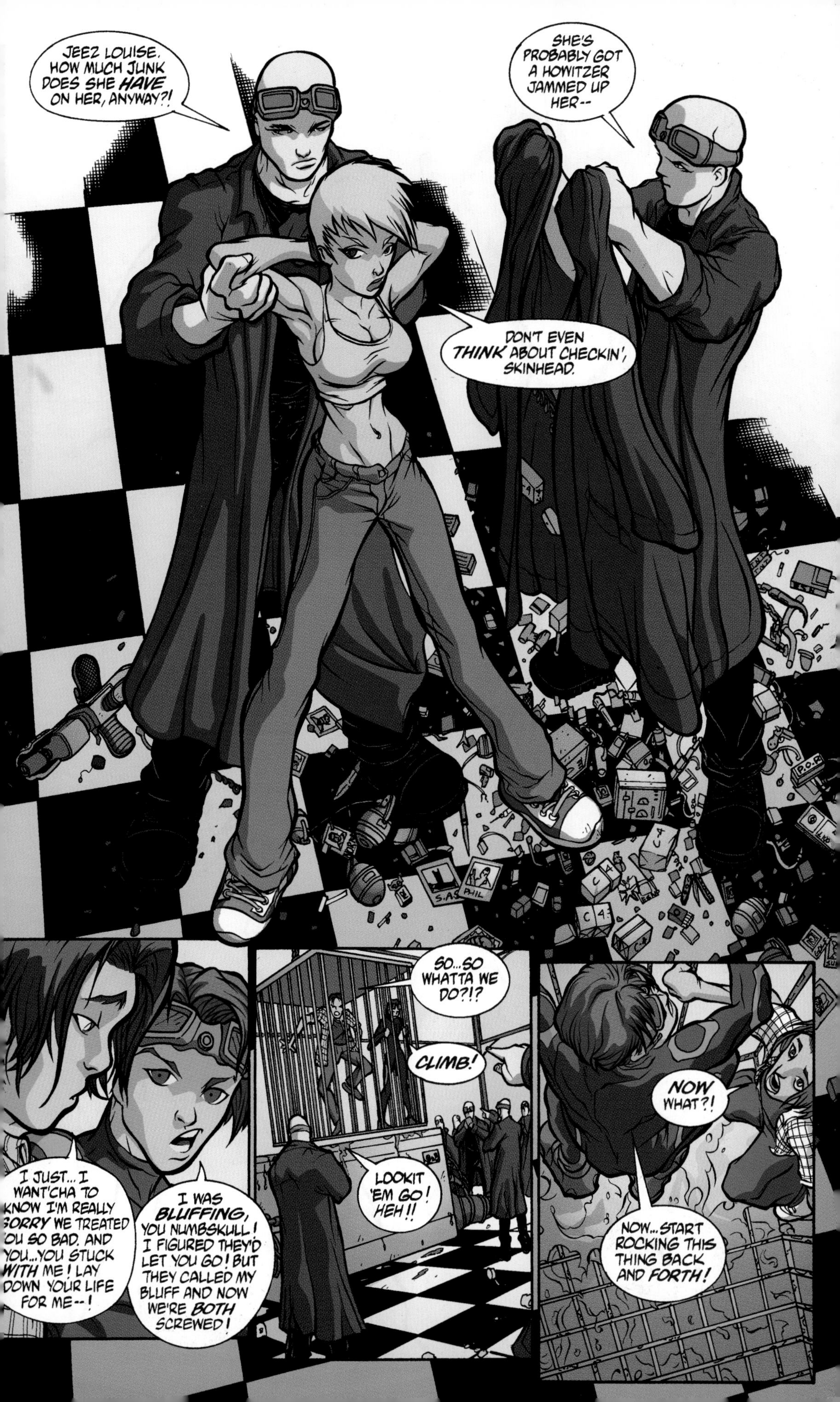
JEEZ LOUISE. HOW MUCH JUNK DOES SHE *HAVE* ON HER, ANYWAY?!
SHE'S PROBABLY GOT A HOWITZER JAMMED UP HER--
DON'T EVEN *THINK* ABOUT CHECKIN', SKINHEAD.
I JUST... I WANT'CHA TO KNOW I'M REALLY *SORRY* WE TREATED YOU SO BAD. AND YOU...YOU STUCK *WITH* ME! LAY DOWN YOUR LIFE FOR ME--!
I WAS *BLUFFING*, YOU NUMBSKULL! I FIGURED THEY'D LET YOU GO! BUT THEY CALLED MY BLUFF AND NOW WE'RE *BOTH* SCREWED!
SO...SO WHATTA WE DO?!?
CLIMB!
LOOKIT 'EM GO! HEH!!
NOW WHAT?!
NOW...START ROCKING THIS THING BACK AND *FORTH*!

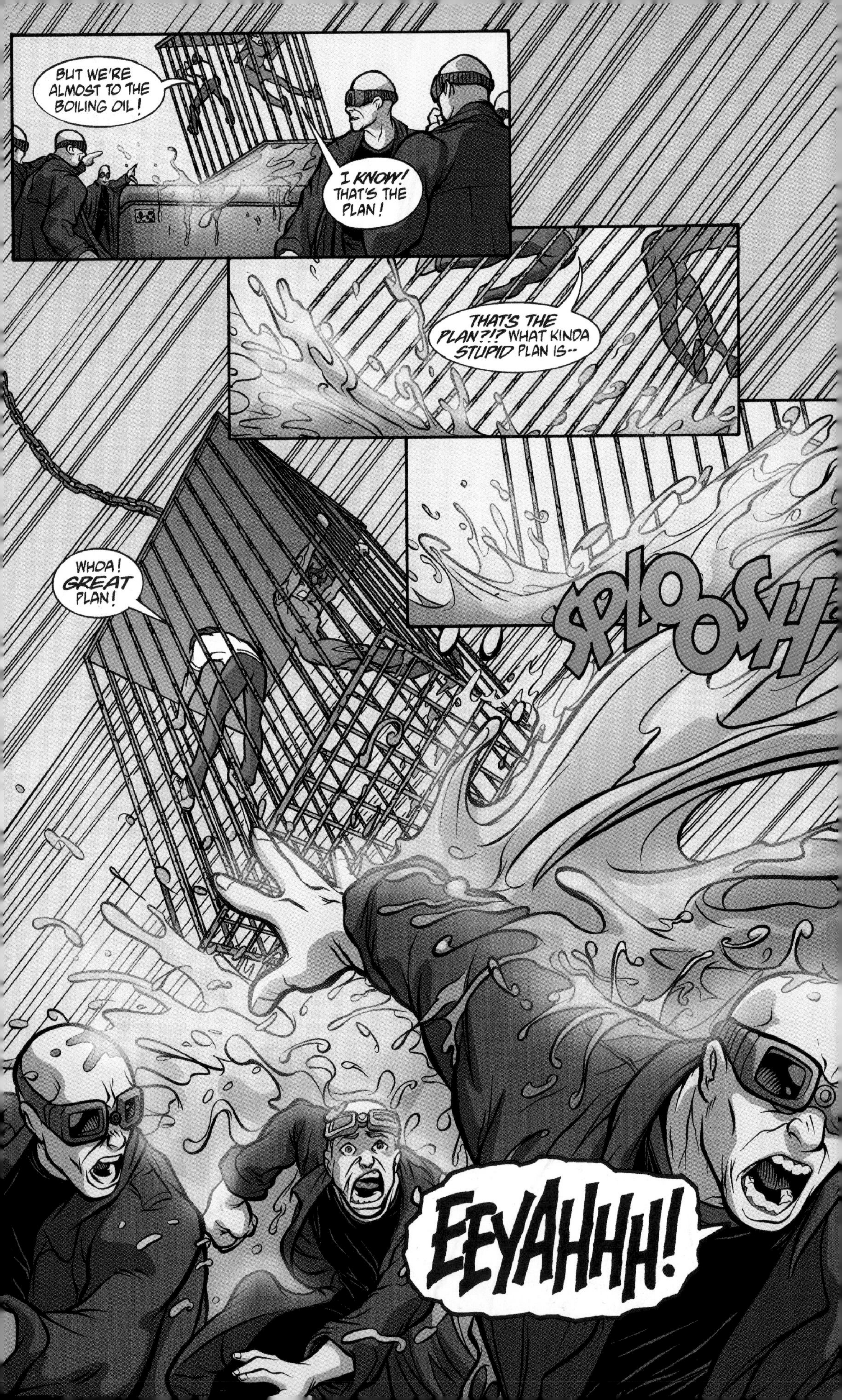
BUT WE'RE ALMOST TO THE BOILING OIL!
I KNOW! THAT'S THE PLAN!
THAT'S THE PLAN?!? WHAT KINDA STUPID PLAN IS--
WHOA! GREAT PLAN!
SPLOOSH
EEYAHHH!

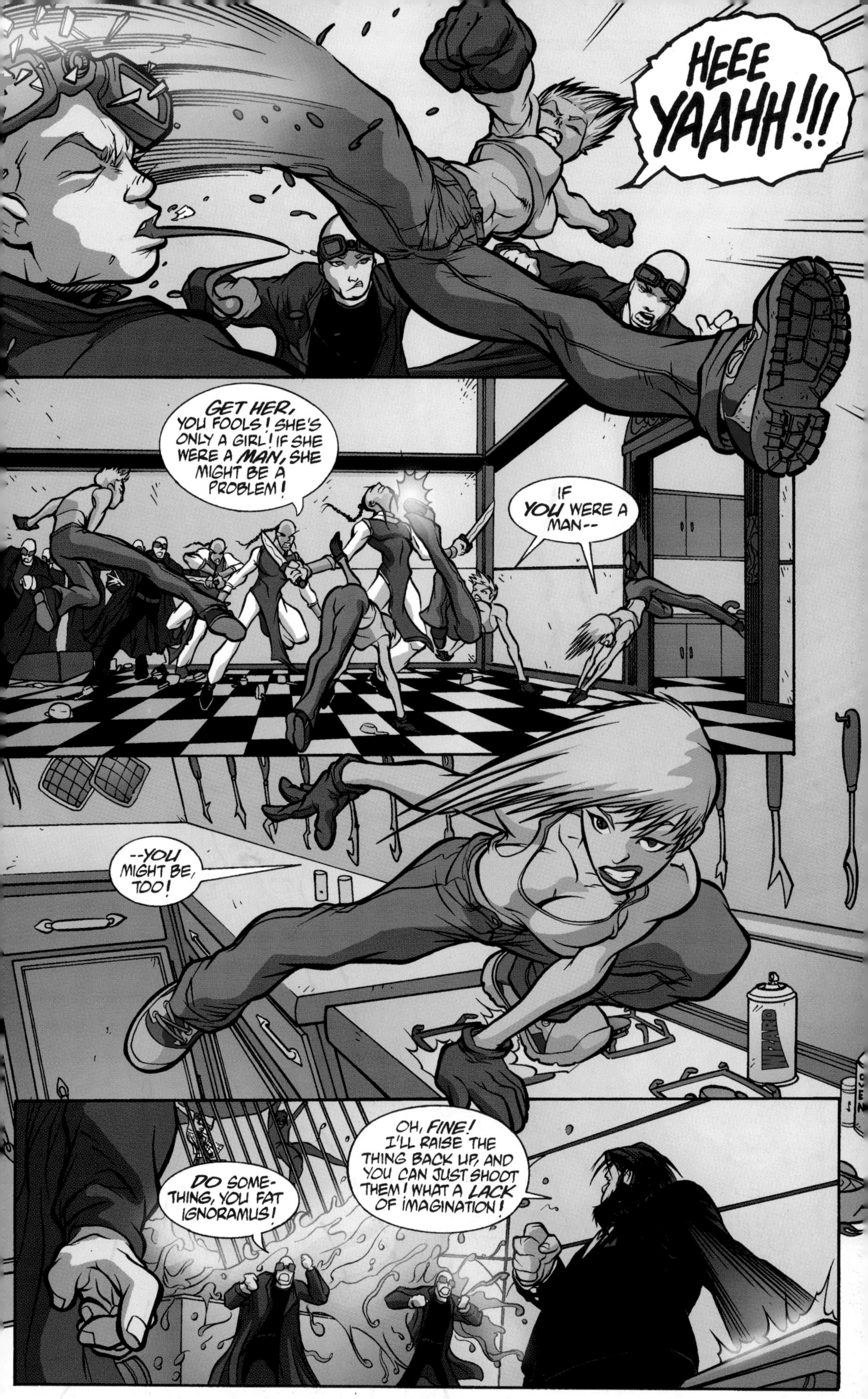
HEEE YAAHH!!!
GET HER, YOU FOOLS! SHE'S ONLY A GIRL! IF SHE WERE A MAN, SHE MIGHT BE A PROBLEM!
IF YOU WERE A MAN--
--YOU MIGHT BE, TOO!
WIZARD
DO SOMETHING, YOU FAT IGNORAMUS!
OH, FINE! I'LL RAISE THE THING BACK UP, AND YOU CAN JUST SHOOT THEM! WHAT A LACK OF IMAGINATION!

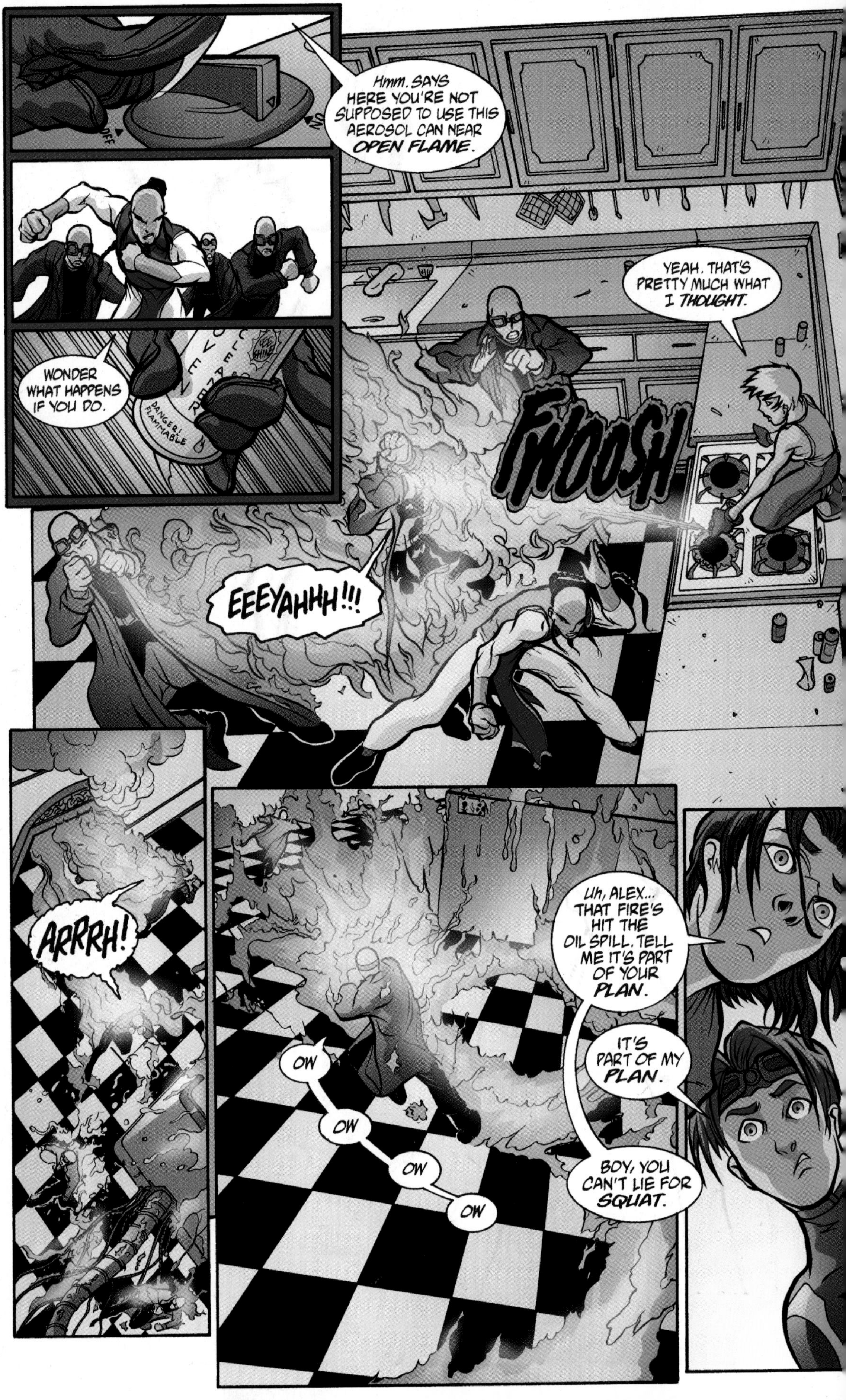
Hmm. SAYS HERE YOU'RE NOT SUPPOSED TO USE THIS AEROSOL CAN NEAR OPEN FLAME.
WONDER WHAT HAPPENS IF YOU DO.
DANGER! FLAMMABLE
YEAH. THAT'S PRETTY MUCH WHAT I THOUGHT.
FWOOSH
EEEYAHHH!!!
ARRRH!
OW
OW
OW
OW
Uh, ALEX... THAT FIRE'S HIT THE OIL SPILL. TELL ME IT'S PART OF YOUR PLAN.
IT'S PART OF MY PLAN.
BOY, YOU CAN'T LIE FOR SQUAT.

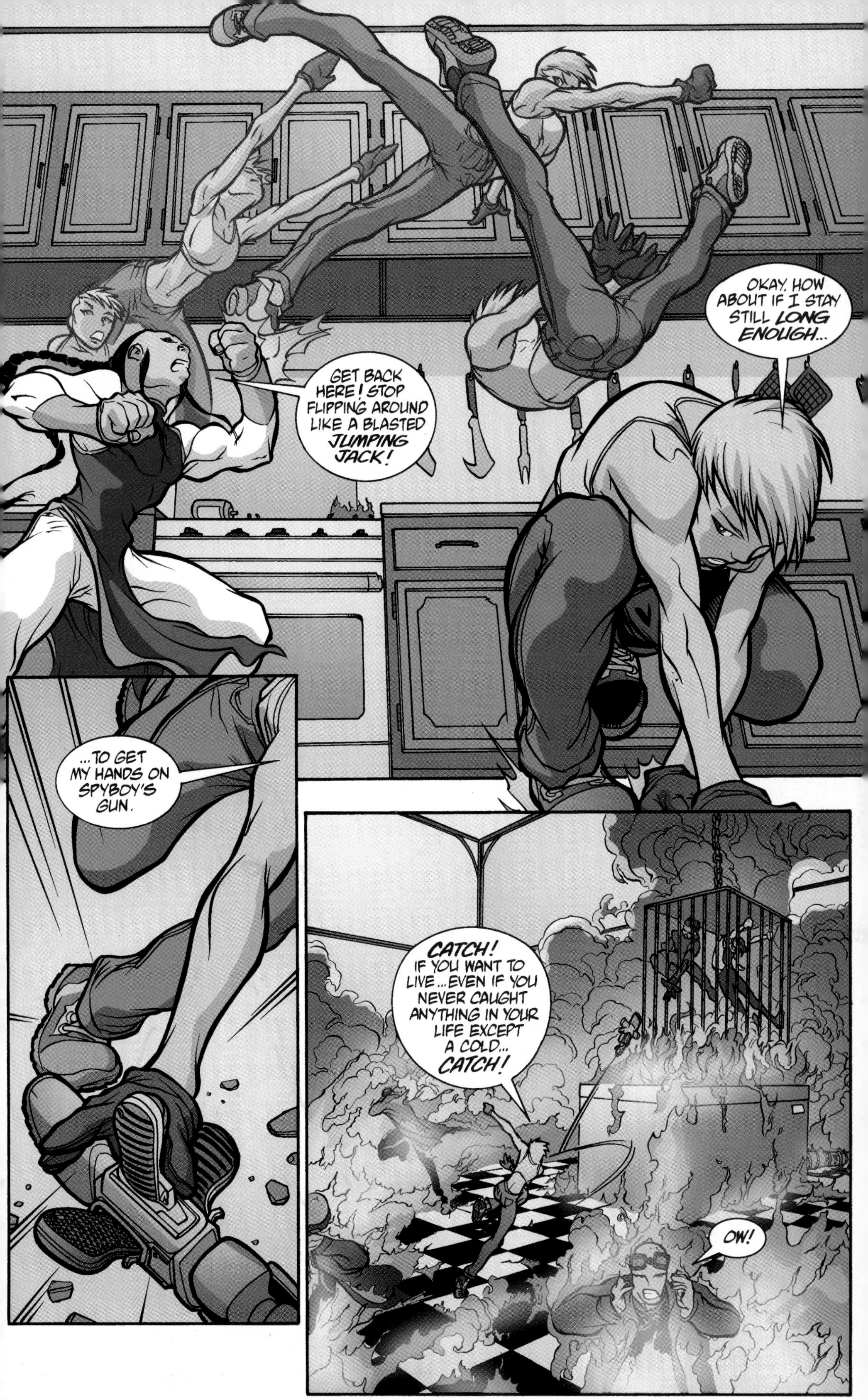
GET BACK HERE! STOP FLIPPING AROUND LIKE A BLASTED JUMPING JACK!
OKAY, HOW ABOUT IF I STAY STILL LONG ENOUGH...
...TO GET MY HANDS ON SPYBOY'S GUN.
CATCH! IF YOU WANT TO LIVE...EVEN IF YOU NEVER CAUGHT ANYTHING IN YOUR LIFE EXCEPT A COLD... CATCH!
OW!

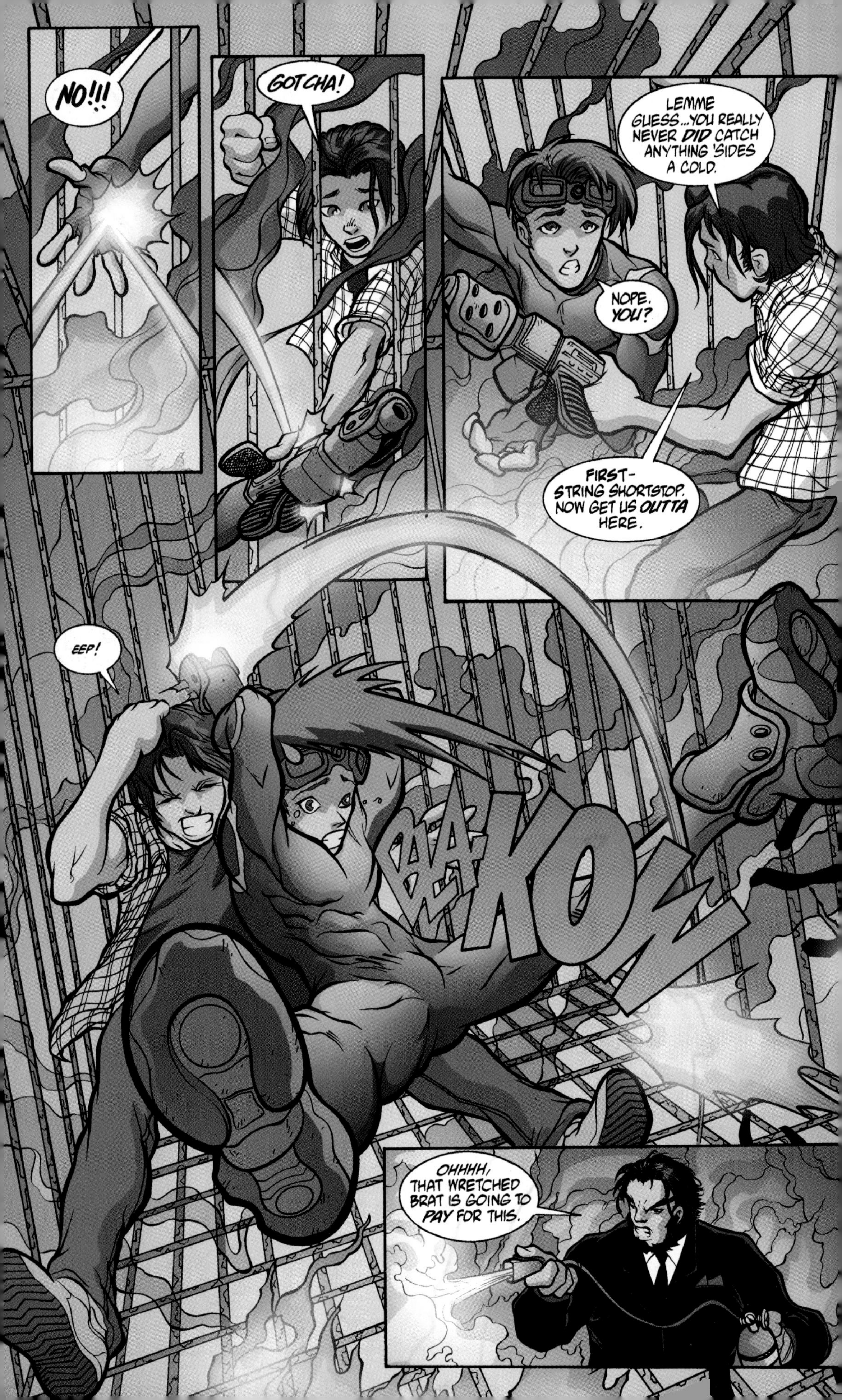
NO!!!
GOTCHA!
LEMME GUESS...YOU REALLY NEVER DID CATCH ANYTHING 'SIDES A COLD.
NOPE. YOU?
FIRST-STRING SHORTSTOP. NOW GET US OUTTA HERE.
EEP!
BA-KOW
OHHHH, THAT WRETCHED BRAT IS GOING TO PAY FOR THIS.

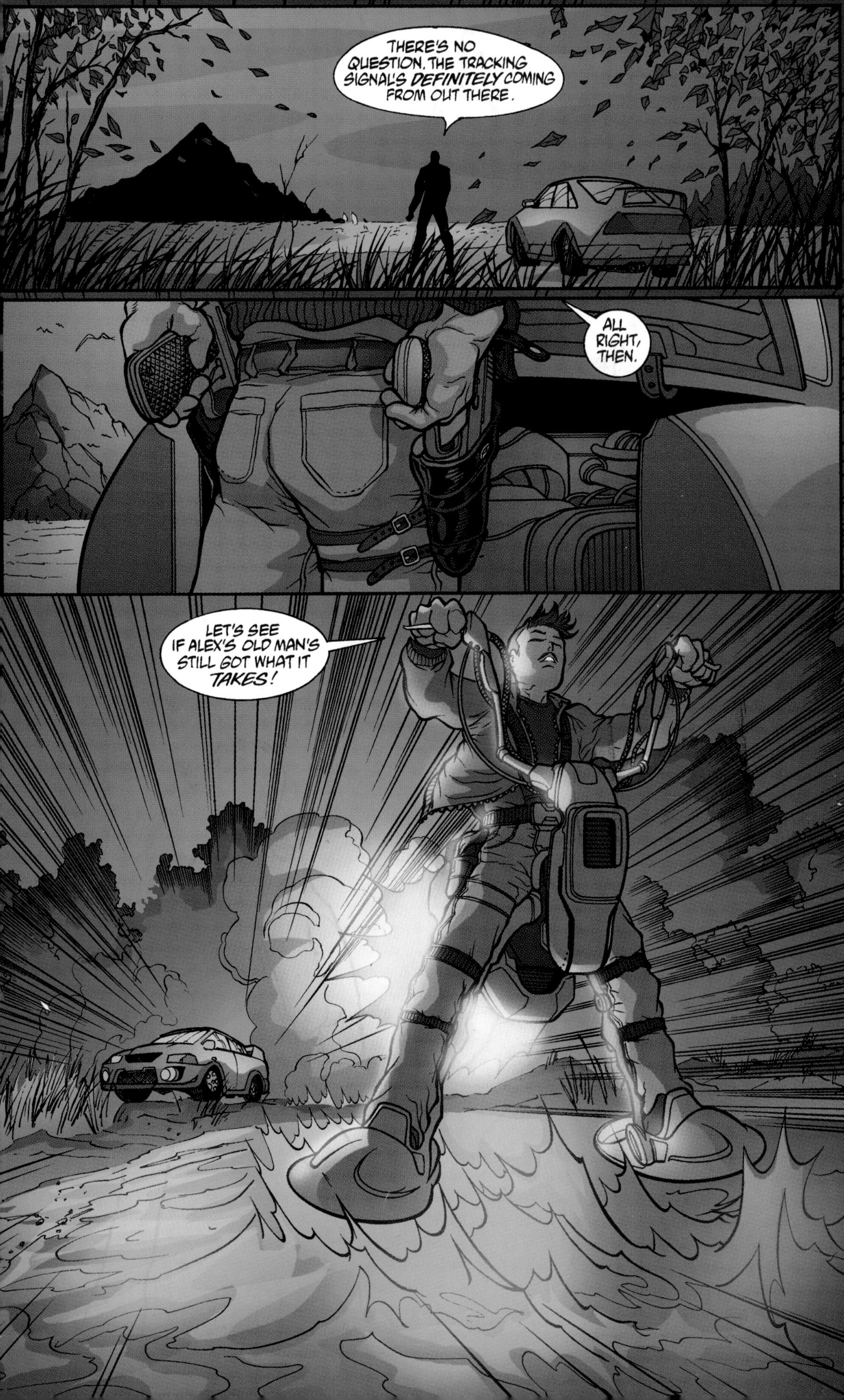
THERE'S NO QUESTION. THE TRACKING SIGNAL'S *DEFINITELY* COMING FROM OUT THERE.
ALL RIGHT, THEN.
LET'S SEE IF ALEX'S OLD MAN'S STILL GOT WHAT IT *TAKES!*

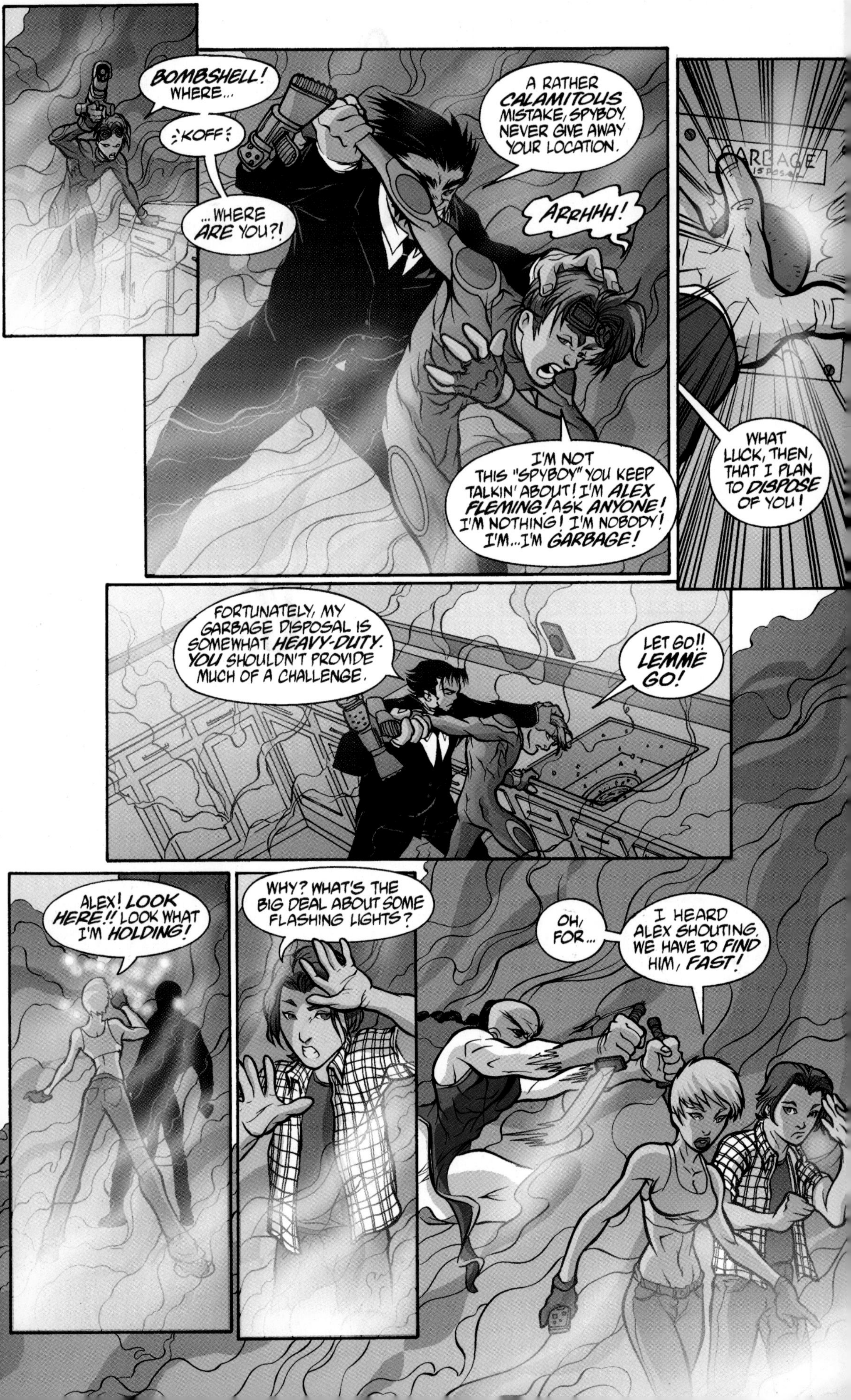

BOMBSHELL! WHERE...
KOFF
...WHERE ARE YOU?!
A RATHER CALAMITOUS MISTAKE, SPYBOY. NEVER GIVE AWAY YOUR LOCATION.
ARRHHH!
I'M NOT THIS "SPYBOY" YOU KEEP TALKIN' ABOUT! I'M ALEX FLEMING! ASK ANYONE! I'M NOTHING! I'M NOBODY! I'M...I'M GARBAGE!
GARBAGE DISPOSAL
WHAT LUCK, THEN, THAT I PLAN TO DISPOSE OF YOU!
FORTUNATELY, MY GARBAGE DISPOSAL IS SOMEWHAT HEAVY-DUTY. YOU SHOULDN'T PROVIDE MUCH OF A CHALLENGE.
LET GO!! LEMME GO!
ALEX! LOOK HERE!! LOOK WHAT I'M HOLDING!
WHY? WHAT'S THE BIG DEAL ABOUT SOME FLASHING LIGHTS?
OH, FOR...
I HEARD ALEX SHOUTING. WE HAVE TO FIND HIM, FAST!

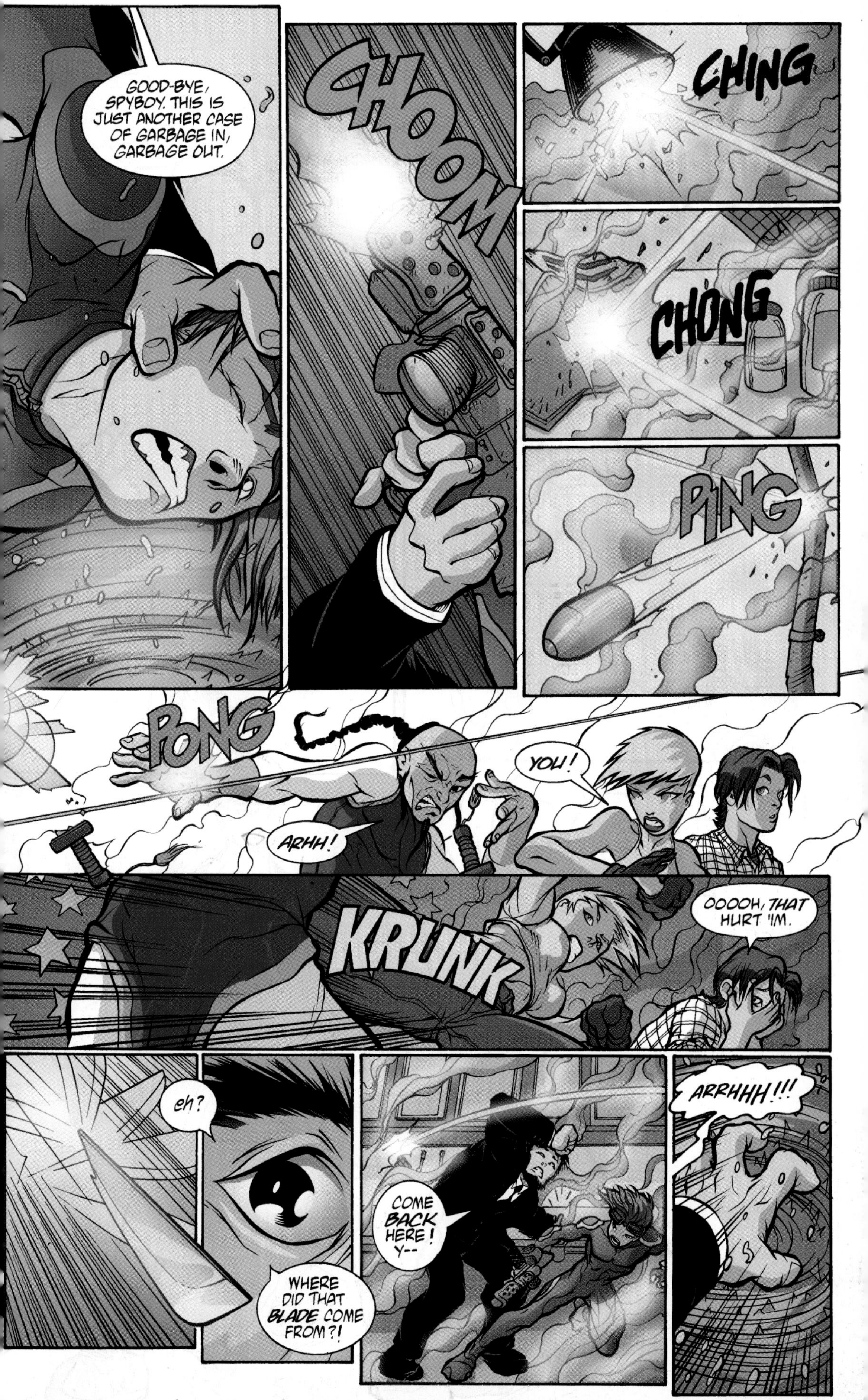
GOOD-BYE, SPYBOY. THIS IS JUST ANOTHER CASE OF GARBAGE IN, GARBAGE OUT.
CHOOM
CHING
CHONG
PING
PONG
YOU!
ARHH!
KRUNK
OOOOH, THAT HURT 'IM.
eh?
WHERE DID THAT BLADE COME FROM?!
COME BACK HERE! Y--
ARRHHH!!!

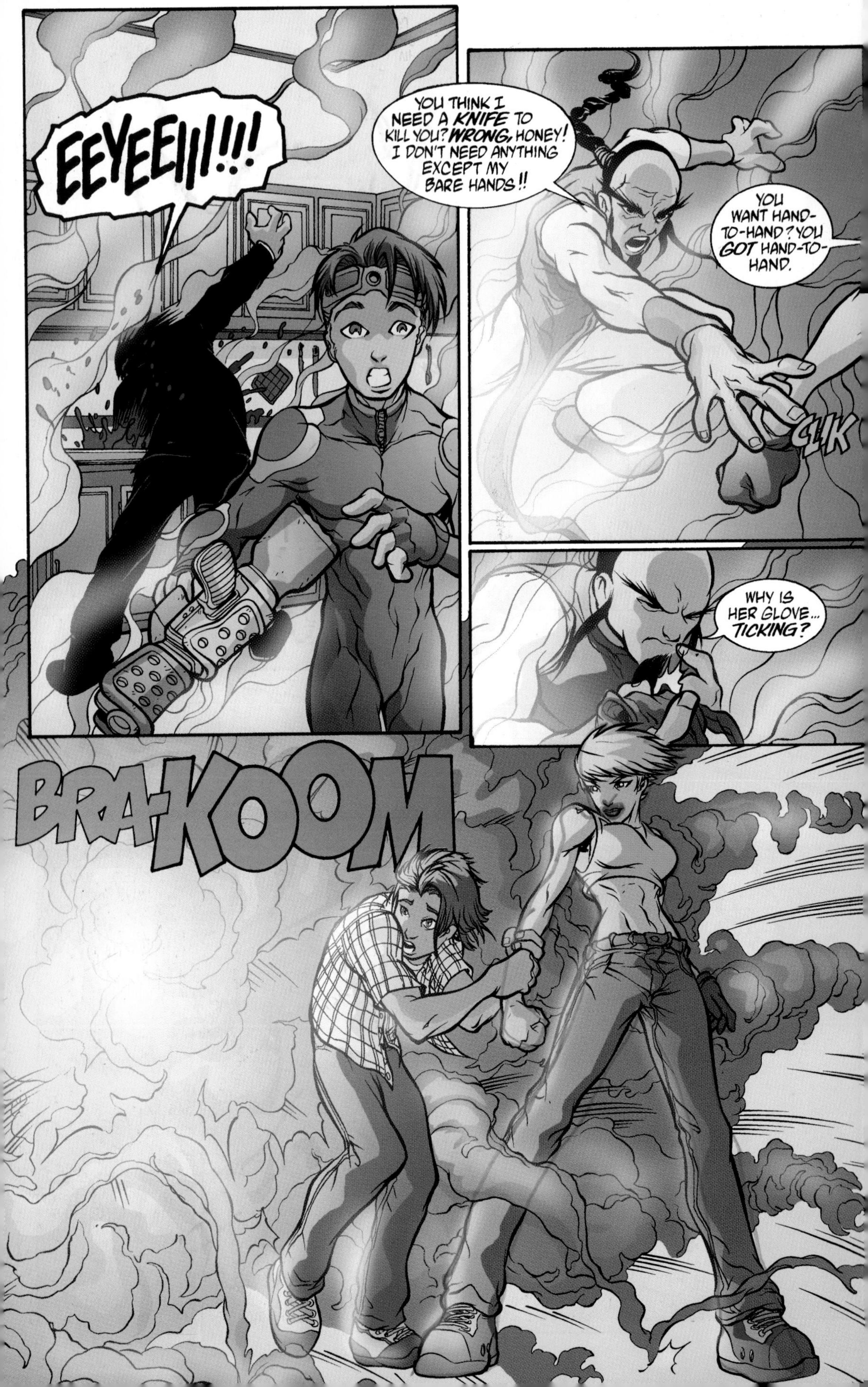

EEYEEIII!!!
YOU THINK I NEED A KNIFE TO KILL YOU? WRONG, HONEY! I DON'T NEED ANYTHING EXCEPT MY BARE HANDS!!
YOU WANT HAND-TO-HAND? YOU GOT HAND-TO-HAND.
CLIK
WHY IS HER GLOVE... TICKING?
BRA-KOOM

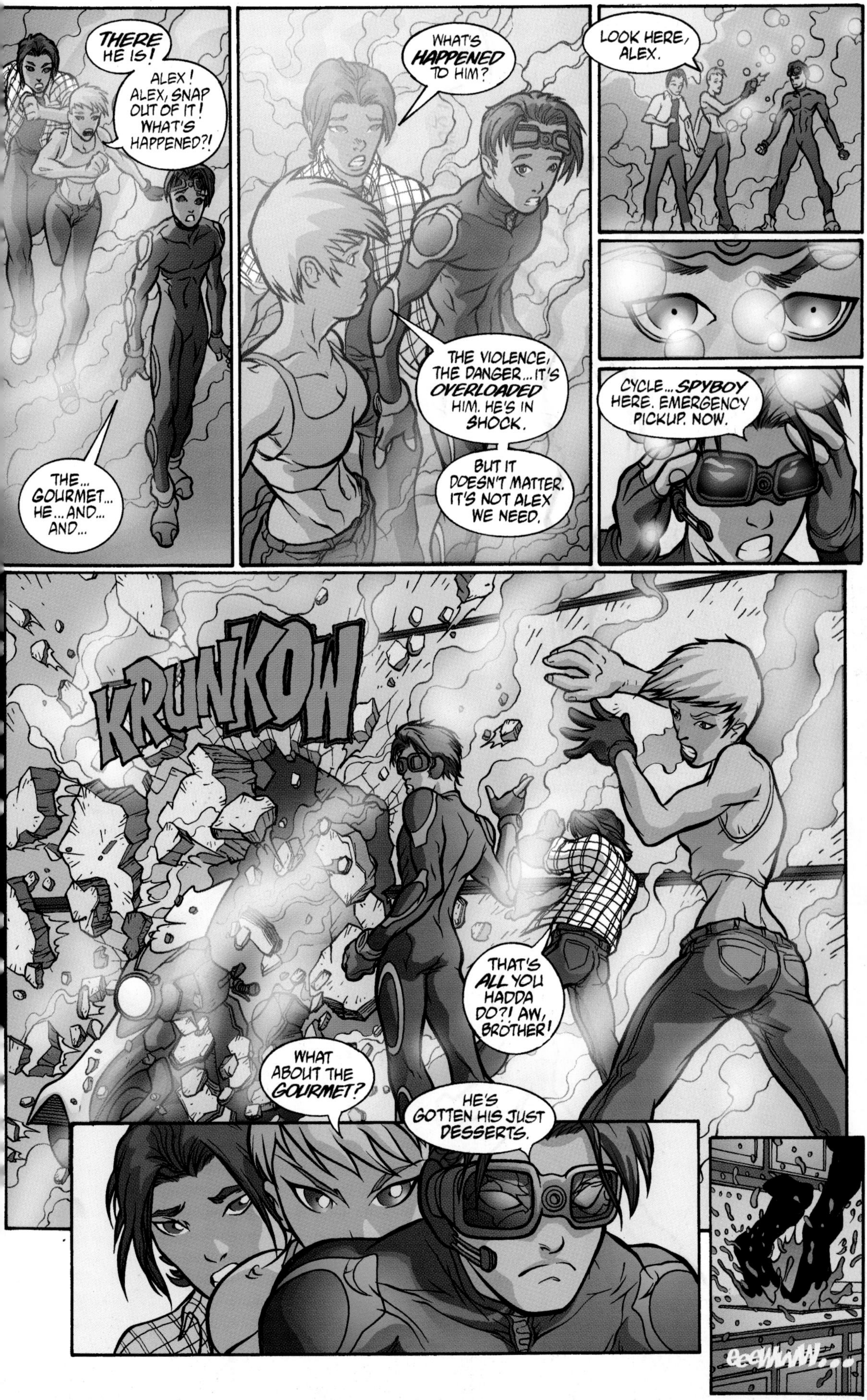
THERE HE IS!
ALEX! ALEX, SNAP OUT OF IT! WHAT'S HAPPENED?!
THE... GOURMET... HE... AND... AND...
WHAT'S HAPPENED TO HIM?
THE VIOLENCE, THE DANGER... IT'S OVERLOADED HIM. HE'S IN SHOCK.
BUT IT DOESN'T MATTER. IT'S NOT ALEX WE NEED.
LOOK HERE, ALEX.
CYCLE... SPYBOY HERE. EMERGENCY PICKUP. NOW.
KRUNKOW
THAT'S ALL YOU HADDA DO?! AW, BROTHER!
WHAT ABOUT THE GOURMET?
HE'S GOTTEN HIS JUST DESSERTS.
eeeWWW...

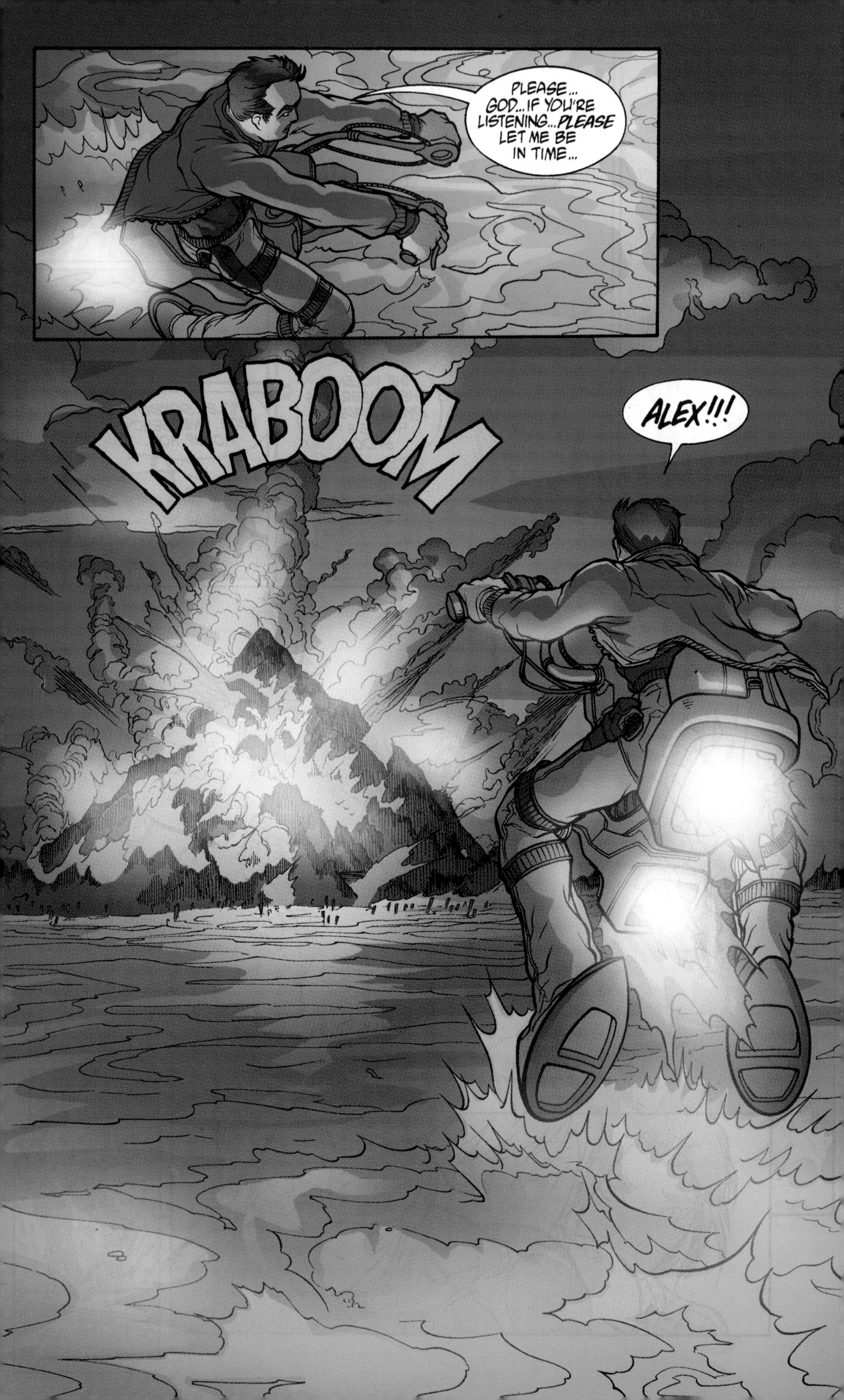
PLEASE... GOD... IF YOU'RE LISTENING... PLEASE LET ME BE IN TIME...
KRABOOM
ALEX!!!

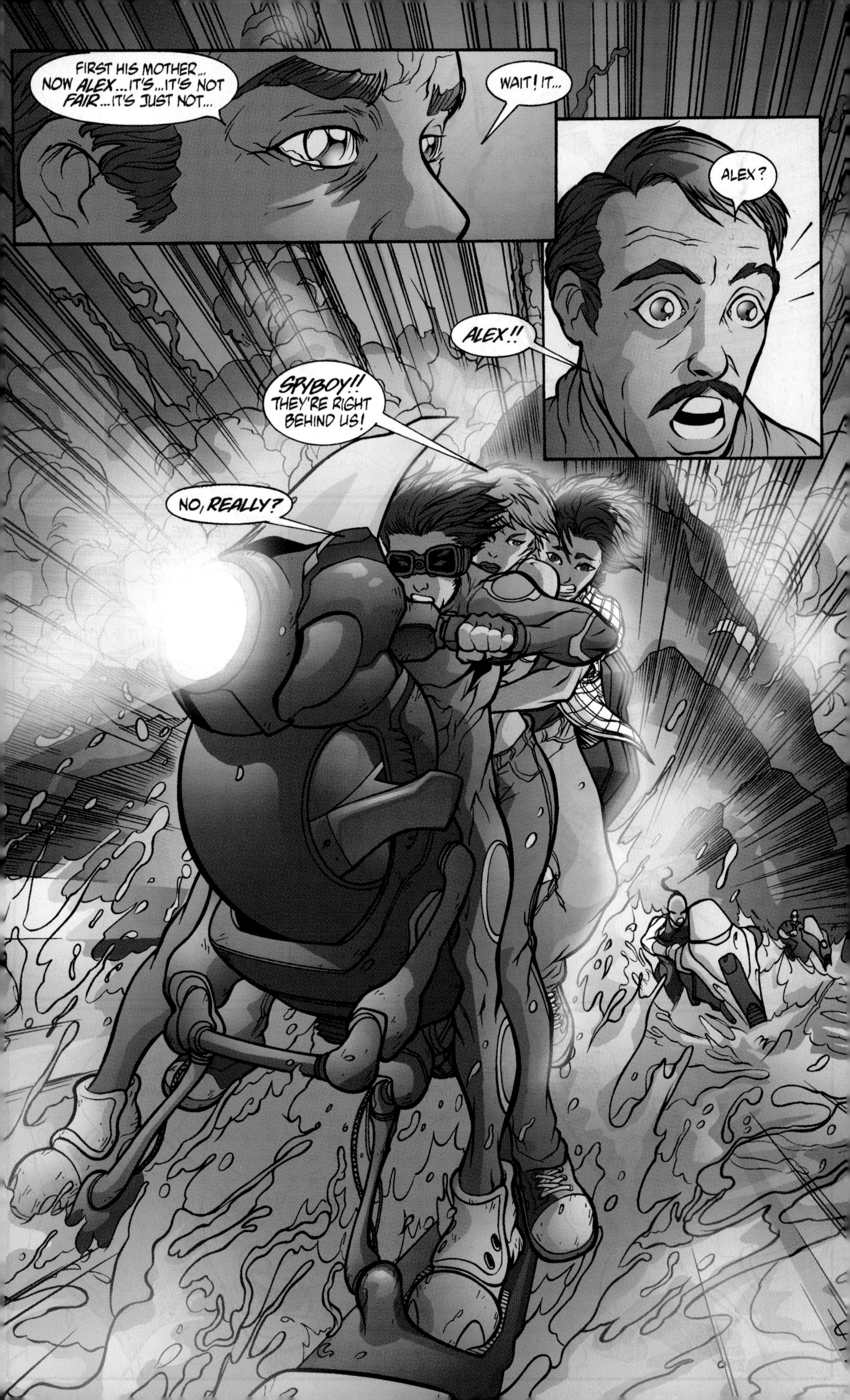
FIRST HIS MOTHER... NOW ALEX...IT'S...IT'S NOT FAIR...IT'S JUST NOT...
WAIT! IT...
ALEX?
ALEX!!
SPYBOY!! THEY'RE RIGHT BEHIND US!
NO, REALLY?

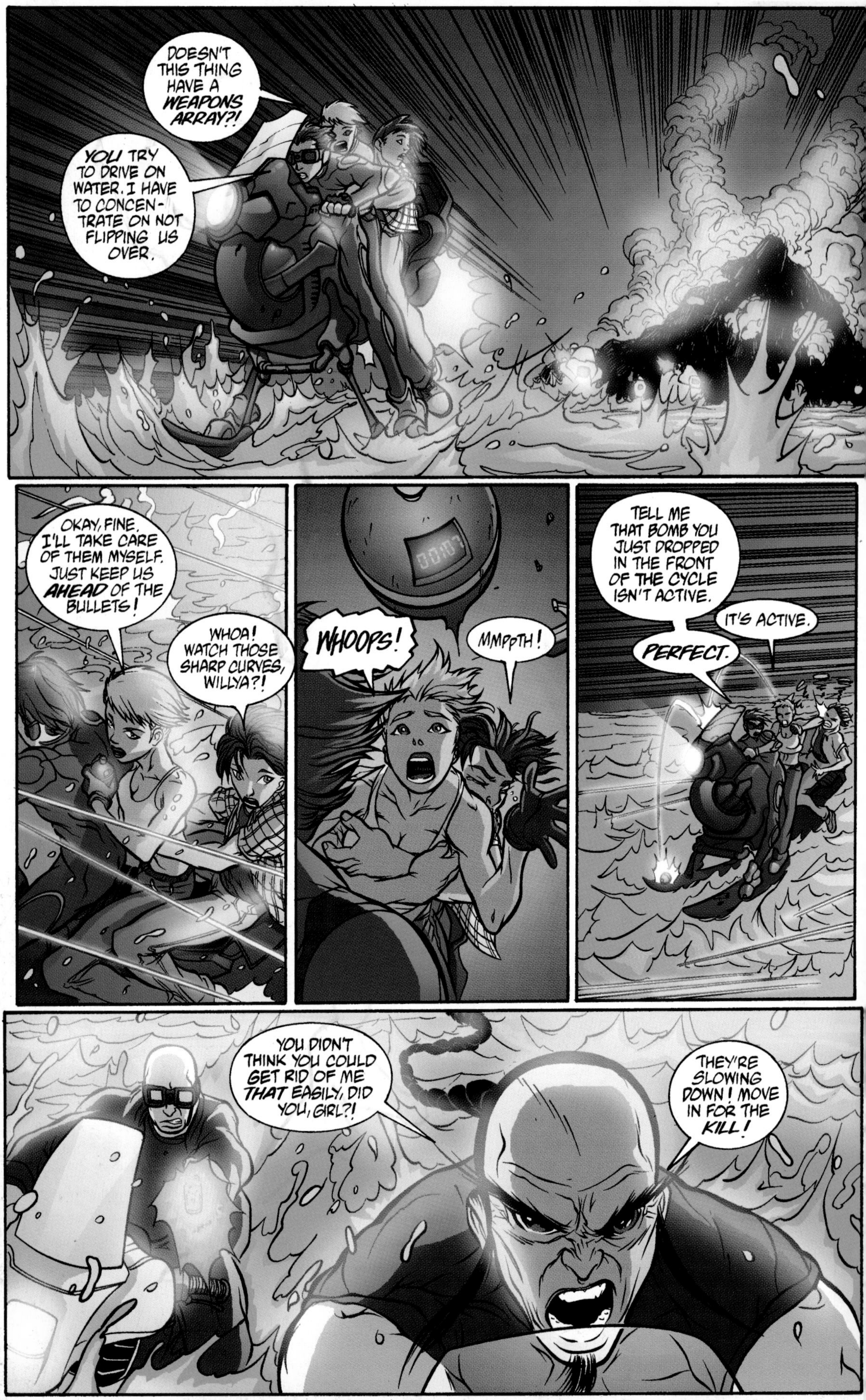
DOESN'T THIS THING HAVE A WEAPONS ARRAY?!
YOU! TRY TO DRIVE ON WATER. I HAVE TO CONCEN-TRATE ON NOT FLIPPING US OVER.
OKAY, FINE. I'LL TAKE CARE OF THEM MYSELF. JUST KEEP US AHEAD OF THE BULLETS!
WHOA! WATCH THOSE SHARP CURVES, WILLYA?!
WHOOPS!
MMPPTH!
TELL ME THAT BOMB YOU JUST DROPPED IN THE FRONT OF THE CYCLE ISN'T ACTIVE.
IT'S ACTIVE.
PERFECT.
YOU DIDN'T THINK YOU COULD GET RID OF ME THAT EASILY, DID YOU, GIRL?!
THEY'RE SLOWING DOWN! MOVE IN FOR THE KILL!

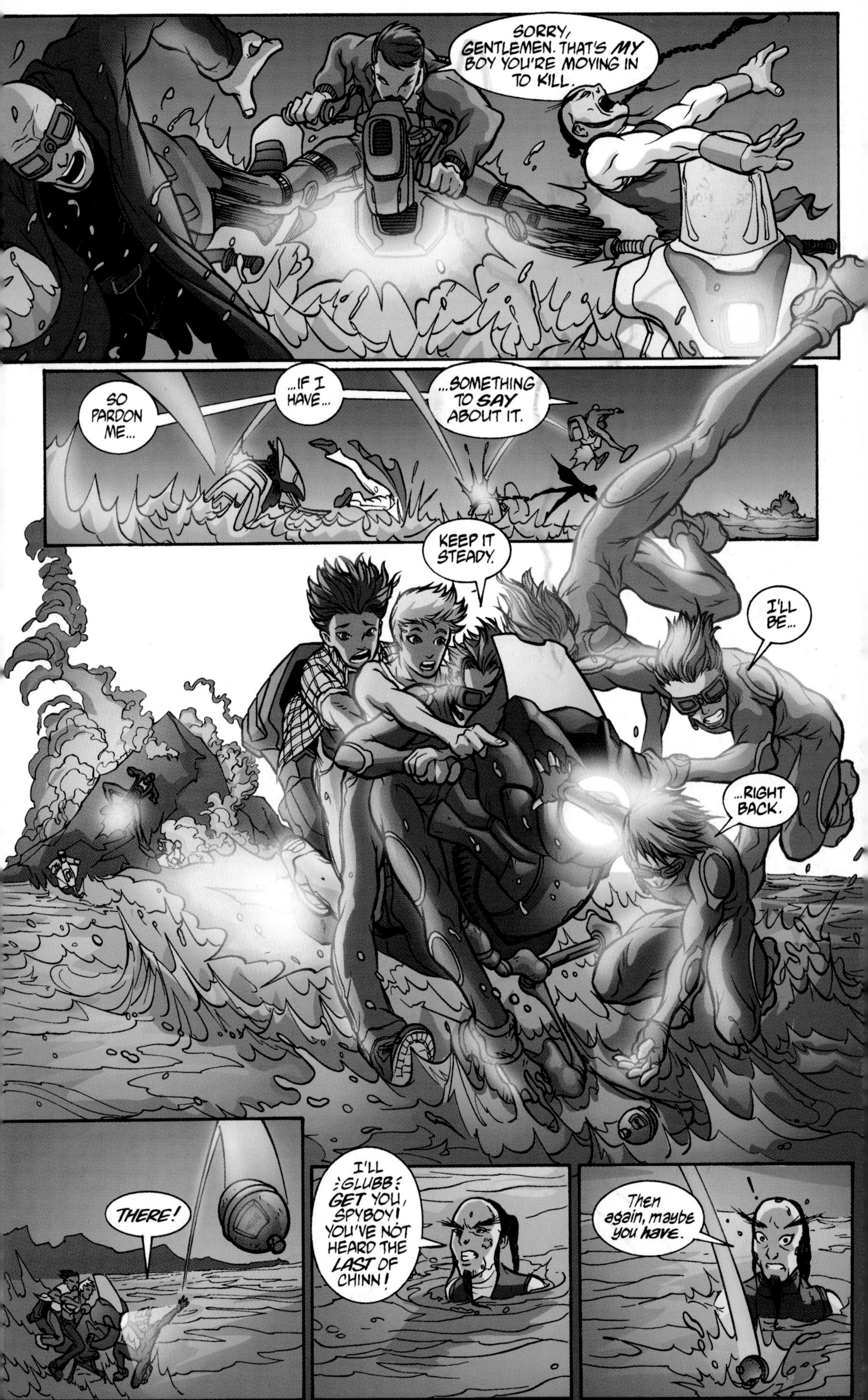
SORRY, GENTLEMEN. THAT'S MY BOY YOU'RE MOVING IN TO KILL.
SO PARDON ME...
...IF I HAVE...
...SOMETHING TO SAY ABOUT IT.
KEEP IT STEADY.
I'LL BE...
...RIGHT BACK.
THERE!
I'LL :GLUBB: GET YOU, SPYBOY! YOU'VE NOT HEARD THE LAST OF CHINN!
Then again, maybe you have.
!

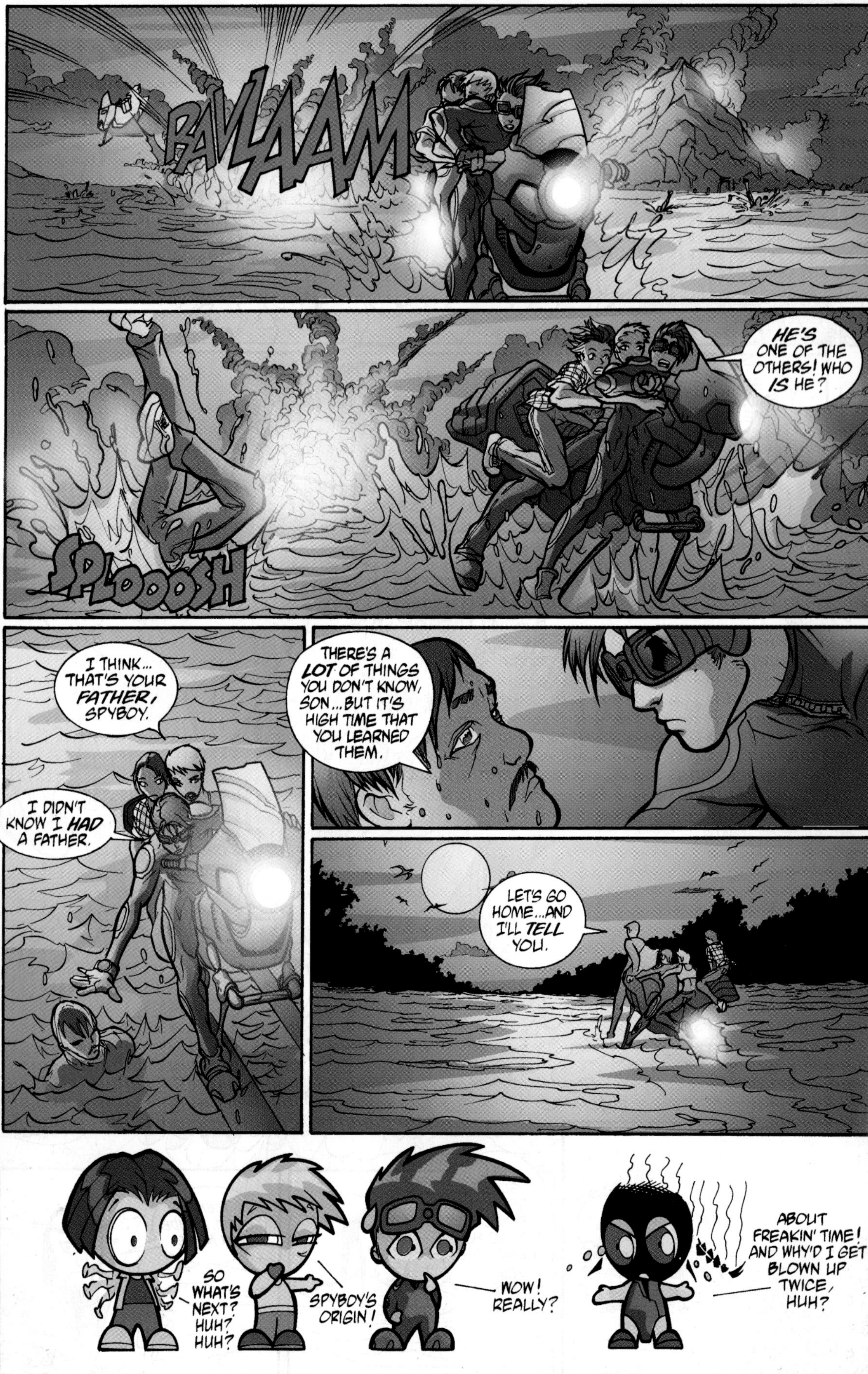
BAVLAAAM
HE'S ONE OF THE OTHERS! WHO IS HE?
SPLOOOSH
I THINK... THAT'S YOUR FATHER, SPYBOY.
I DIDN'T KNOW I HAD A FATHER.
THERE'S A LOT OF THINGS YOU DON'T KNOW, SON... BUT IT'S HIGH TIME THAT YOU LEARNED THEM.
LET'S GO HOME...AND I'LL TELL YOU.
SO WHAT'S NEXT? HUH? HUH?
SPYBOY'S ORIGIN!
WOW! REALLY?
ABOUT FREAKIN' TIME! AND WHY'D I GET BLOWN UP TWICE, HUH?